[illegible] 1996

From Guy

Mountain Chronicles

Jon Whyte

Mountain Chronicles

Jon Whyte

A Collection of Columns on
the Canadian Rockies
from the Banff *Crag and Canyon*
1975 - 1991

EDITED BY Brian Patton

Altitude Publishing
BANFF ALBERTA CANADA
1992

Canadian Cataloguing in Publication Data
Whyte, Jon, 1941-1992
Mountain Chronicles
Essays originally published 1975-1991 in the weekly newspaper *Crag & Canyon*
ISBN 0-919381-89-8
1. Rocky Mountains, Canadian (B.C. and Alta.) – History.*
2. Rocky Mountains, Canadian (B.C. and Alta.) – Social life and customs.*
3. Rocky Mountains, Canadian (B.C. and Alta.) – Description and travel.*
I. Title.
FC 219.W59 1992   971.1   C92-091642-2   F1090.W59 1992

Front cover photograph of Jon Whyte by Robert W. Sandford
Design: Robert MacDonald, MediaClones Inc.
Contributing Editor: John Ricker
Proofreader: Catherine Ludgate
Printed in Canada on acid-free paper at D.W. Friesen, Altona Manitoba

This book was published with the assistance of the
Alberta Foundation for the Literary Arts, and Alberta Culture

Altitude Publishing Ltd.
POST OFFICE BOX 490
BANFF ALBERTA CANADA TOL OCO

INTRODUCTION

In the spring of 1968, at age 27, Jon Whyte returned to his boyhood home of Banff from Stanford University. He planned on using the Canadian Rockies as a setting for a film documentary which would satisfy his thesis requirement for a Masters degree in Communications. With a Masters in Medieval English from the University of Alberta already in hand, there was little reason to believe that he would linger in this tiny mountain resort community after the production was complete. But linger he did, and over the next twenty-three years, until his death in 1992, he was a dominant presence in matters literary, cultural, and environmental in Banff and the Rockies.

Jon's success as a mountain writer, both as a poet and essayist, can be attributed to the unique environment in which he was raised. He was born in Banff on March 15, 1941. His father was Dave "Jack" Whyte, Jr., son of Dave and Annie Curren White who were both early settlers in the Bow Valley and prominent citizens of Banff. His mother was Barbara Carpenter Whyte, a school teacher who was raised in a Quaker family in the eastern United States. From his father's side of the family he inherited a strong sense of place and history, from his mother a love of books and the English language. And then there was his uncle and aunt, Peter and Catharine Whyte, living next door in a beautiful log home which also served as a studio for these two full-time landscape and portrait artists.

It was a very special place to grow into, this still-peaceful mountain resort of Banff in the 1940s and 50s, with pioneer outfitters and guides for neighbors, Stoney Natives as family friends and frequent visitors, and homes filled with books and art.

In 1956 Jon moved to Medicine Hat, Alberta, with his mother and finished his secondary education there. In the autumn of 1959 he entered the University of Alberta in Edmonton. The years between his entrance and the spring of 1967, when he completed his Masters degree, were some of the most exciting and stimulating in the university's history. It was in the university's English department that Jon began his writing career and his long association with many of Canada's most respected poets and authors. And, finally, there was Palo Alto, California, and nine months of American cultural immersion at Stanford.

Outside of Banff, Jon was best known as a poet and regional historian. He published several volumes of poetry, contributed poems to a number of anthologies, and produced work for performance on CBC Radio. Historical works which he authored or co-authored included books on Lake Louise, Lake O'Hara, Indians of the Rockies, and wildlife artist Carl Rungius. But within the community of Banff and the Bow Corridor, Jon Whyte the writer was best known for his weekly columns in the *Summit News* and *Crag and Canyon* newspapers.

I met Jon shortly after his return to Banff in 1968 when we were employed at the Banff Book and Art Den. We had both dabbled in journalism at university, so when local publisher Jack Gorman was looking for writers to fill space in his new weekly, the *Summit News*, we happily joined his team. While I was content to churn out news stories, features, and editorials, Jon was more selective. Standard newspaper journalism held little interest for him, so he limited himself to a weekly column and the occasional arts review. His first column appeared on October 31, 1968, under the heading of "Column ... Jon Whyte." A month later he added the name "Ra/umblings." In all, he wrote 69 columns for the *Summit News*.

It may seem as rather modest ambition for one possessed of Jon's talents to bother with a regular column in a small town weekly. Yet, Jack Gorman's *Summit News* was a liberal newspaper operating in one of western Canada's most cosmopolitan small towns. Jon was allowed to write as he pleased on just about any subject that might rise to the surface of his highly eclectic mind, and he could criticize the pro-growth factions in the community in a manner that would have been unheard of in most small town periodicals.

Jon established his reputation as a dedicated observer of mountains when he added a weekly piece called "Whyte's Weather" in the spring of 1969. In addition to collecting the weekly weather statistics from the local weather office, he produced a haiku to portray the mood of each day as he had observed it:

Sunday, April 13
Totterdemalion
day of spring fooferaw –
rain, shine, sleet, snow, sun.
High 49, Low 34, Prec. tr.

Monday, April 28
Humdrum or hohum
anyway a day so grey
made most of it glum.
High 58, Low 30, Prec. 0

Thursday, May 1
Rain thickens a day
as it falls darkening all
to wet slick midnight.
High 53, Low 34, Prec. tr.

Sunday, May 4
No spectacular effect
except Rundle
crowned with forgotten stars.
High 51, Low 35, Prec. 0

Jon concocted this off-beat project, I am sure, as a means of practising his craft and honing his powers of nature observation. He proposed to carry on with the experiment for a year, but after the weather column and his hard-won haiku were sacrificed from a couple of issues due to space requirements, he abandoned the endeavor.

In 1970 the *Summit News* collapsed after an exhausting four-year battle with the venerable *Crag and Canyon*. Jon's style of writing was far too liberal and unorthodox for then *Crag and Canyon* editor Bill McCusker, so for the next few years he busied himself with other projects.

In 1974 the *Crag and Canyon* was sold to Pat and Stephanie Boswell. In the autumn of that year they were shopping for an editor and I hired on to take over the position in January. With the promise of a "new look" *Crag and Canyon*, Jon offered his services as a columnist. On October 16, 1974, his column "Where Man and Mountain Meet" first appeared in the *Crag*.

Jon and I only worked together on the paper for three months. The vicissitudes of editing a small town weekly soon proved my undoing. But Jon stayed on and, over the next sixteen years, he wrote 819 columns. During that time span he missed only a few weeks, usually when he was travelling abroad, then reruns or guest columns appeared in the space.

The title of the column came from a William Blake line: "Great things are done when man and mountains meet; that is not done by jostling in the street." When he changed the name of the column to

"When Peaks and People Meet" in 1987 (out of deference to the feminist movement), he reconsidered the quote:

Nice little bit of writing, Mr. Blake. I like it for its fulcrum force, placing those who prefer peaks and people on one side of the balance, those who like jostle on the other. As the jostle factor (Banff Ave. and ultra large resorts, for example) goes up, the possibility of "great things" goes down. As one lowers the jostle factor, the possibility of great things goes up.

It was a perspective which emerged in many of his columns.

Unlike most newspaper columnists who try to develop a readership through predictability of topic, Jon's writing became even more eclectic at the *Crag* than it was at the *Summit News*. On any given week he could be writing about the vagaries of mountain weather, the sorry state of Alberta politics, a hike to a mountain fire lookout, an art exhibit or play at the Banff Centre, an appreciation of one of Banff's pioneers, a trip to a writers' conference in Edmonton or Toronto, the threat of commercial development in the Kananaskis Valley, a new book by Annie Dillard or Octavio Paz, a family ski trip to Skoki Lodge, the art purchasing policy of the National Gallery, or the joys of watching ravens.

In a column written in late 1990, Jon mused over all this variety: "In writing a thousand or so of these columns I have covered a diversity of topic material very few people other than my mother remember. I don't have an index to them, so finding out what I may have said – and when I may have said it – is a task that I consider unworthy of everybody's time."

This sort of diversity was pretty heady stuff for a small town like Banff. While the community was sophisticated enough to provide an audience for the topic-of-the-week no matter how esoteric it might be, there were few who could appreciate or comprehend every offering. As a result of this, and the occasional column which simply played with words or puns, Jon's column acquired a reputation among some *Crag* subscribers as being unreadable by anyone with a sub-genius IQ.

In reality, most of Jon's columns were accessible to anyone capable of reading the English language, and many were all too readable for those in the town who didn't agree with his liberal political views or his strong anti-growth advocacy for the town of Banff.

On February 21, 1991, Jon wrote his last column for the *Crag and Canyon*. There was a strong note of bitterness and disillusionment in this final piece:

The ledger can make one feel useless. Twenty years ago, the balance of summer and winter visitation, facilities and housing, and services and demand was even, and the town had a healthy sensibility. How did matters get so out of shape? How did the community of Banff allow itself to be so weak-willed that it did not rise up again and again against the villainies and injustices which I and so many other people felt were eroding the spirit of the town?

Had I written about each nick of the death of a thousand nicks – while recognizing that some of them have been swipes, gashes, slashes, gouges, and lacerations – that have weakened the Banff that used to be, I would not have had time to reflect on the real joys that can exist here.

The break was designed as a sabbatical which would allow him time to complete a history of the town of Banff. It was through this project that he hoped to discover "why matters deteriorated ... and why such an ethical and moral vacuum developed here." It was a book which was never finished. On January 6, 1992, Jon Whyte died of cancer in the Banff Mineral Springs Hospital.

So, what to make of all this Sunday morning scribbling? What justification for resurrecting a selection of 600 word (more or less) newspaper columns in book form? Quite simply, many of Jon's offerings surmount their humble origins. They are wonderful essays which capture the spirit of life in these mountains as well as anything that has ever been written. In an interview which he gave to the *Crag* in 1991, a few months after writing his last column, Jon was asked if he missed writing his column. "It's nice five times a year," he said, "because there are things five times a year that are topical. Forty-five times a year you are filling space."

From my own perusal of the more than 800 columns which he wrote for the *Crag*, I would say that this estimate is fairly accurate. Most weeks were devoted to rather straightforward concerns, the sort of issue-raising and idle musing which occupies most columnists. But because he was always an observer of nature, mountains, and the state of humankind, he would frequently bring forth an inspired piece of surpassing quality.

But what did Jon think of this long, persistent effort in the pages of his hometown newspaper? In a column published September 2, 1987, he wrote:

But then I don't write this material just to let off steam or pass along my point of view on issues confronting the community ... I increasingly think of my brief essays in the mode which Bart Robinson suggested quite a while back. These writings aren't history or meditation or rhapsody. But they have become a chronicle of this place which is our place.

A chronicle of this place. And as such, these writings have much in common with the journals of another writer who Jon greatly admired – Henry David Thoreau. Indeed, Jon's life had many parallels with that of Thoreau's: returning from a prestigious university to live out his life in a small hometown; a keen observer of nature with a strong attachment to the landscape of home; a relentless social critic who frequently offended and infuriated the village folk; a bachelor all his life; an early death. One might even find similarities in his gaunt, angular features and somewhat stern reproving countenance. And then there was Jon's Aunt Catharine, very much his spiritual patron; it should not seem out of place that she was born and raised in Concord, Massachusetts.

But enough of this. Back to Jon:

It's tricky, this business of writing with one eye on the wheel of history while the other is on the issue of the moment, and in my diffidence, I'm just as likely to suggest that writing for a newspaper is an easier and quicker way of writing on water. After all the Latin name for the newspaper of the Romans' day was ephemerides, *the root for our word ephemeral. And in the world of blat and bugle, it's equally wise to remember that the Italian name for newspaper is gazette, out of the same stem as* gazza, *the Italian magpie.*

Mayflies and magpies: the north and south of the newspaper. But then I also remember the gentle and wise essays which appeared in The Spectator *and* The Tatler, *parts of a newspaper tradition which are readable two centuries later. I always say to people who suggest my columns should be collected and published that I don't write 'em for that purpose. I put the durable stuff into my books. For a good time, read my poetry.*

And I can only say to my old friend, "Forgiveness, Horst." In the week before you died, I started collecting these columns from the back issues of the *Crag*, perhaps as displacement therapy, a break from the long hospital vigil. But as I went along and reread these pieces from this pivotal period in the history of our valley, I became convinced that they are every bit as gentle and wise as the entries in Thoreau's journals or Pepys' diaries, and often a lot more fun. They should be available for those who missed them when they were first published.

And for the rest of us, we should read them once more and have them accessible, for they provide an important chronicle of this place. Our place.

* * *

In selecting these pieces for publication, I have not included any columns from Jon's *Summit News* days. Though many of the themes were the same in those early writings, they did not possess the polish and essay quality which emerged in the post-1974 *Crag and Canyon* period. I believe that Jon's facility with words matured in the early 1970s through his own increased activity in writing poetry, his reading of nature writers like Edward Abbey and Annie Dillard, and, perhaps, through his close association with his Aunt Catharine – a gentle and wise woman if there ever was one.

I have stuck with columns which have mountain themes and have tried to include a good mix of what was best in Jon's writings: nature essays, childhood memories of Banff, appreciations of mountain pioneers, contemporary tales, humourous fantasies, and a smattering of biting social commentary. I have passed over some good pieces in order to keep a fairly even spread through the sixteen year period.

These columns are reproduced here as he wrote them, and with the elimination of the insidious typos that appeared in many of the *Crag* originals.

Not every reader will be familiar with all of the Banff characters who crop up in some of these columns. I have not identified any of these people, believing that their role and importance in the region will be evident. As Jon would have said, "If you want more information, go to the Archives and look 'em up."

I would like to thank Stephen Hutchings for his interest in producing a book of Jon's writing and for accepting my opinion that these pieces are worthy of publication.

Thanks also to Don Bourdon, Lena Goon, Alex Huculak, and Mary Andrews of the Whyte Museum of the Canadian Rockies who assisted me in the task of photocopying these selections.

And a special thanks to Carol Black who offered support and advice through the process of compiling this book, and for her comments on this introduction.

And finally, my deepest appreciation to Jon's mother Barbara Carpenter Whyte, his brother Harold, and all other members of the Whyte/White family who gave me their permission and support to proceed with this book.

BRIAN PATTON

Last winter was the winter of the ravens. When the snow is deeper, later in the winter, they may be back.

Ravens were never seen in town a while back. Crows were common, and magpies too, but the great black splendour of the raven was not among our prizes. Rumour says they're up at the dump, rattling their throats and sharpening their sabres, and I hope it's true: I've come to love those great shaggy birds.

When we were kids we entertained the possibility of catching a crow, splitting its tongue, teaching it to swear, and letting it fly about the school where it would say aloud for us the things we dared only whisper. What would you do with a crow?

We never caught a crow. Because we were ardent citizens of the national park? No, the national park idea came up in our education infrequently, if ever, and it was only the bear, moose and deer wandering about the town who defended the national park. Have things changed? I doubt that the national park comes up in classes frequently even now. If I'm wrong I'll eat crow.

No, we never caught a crow. It's a tough thing to catch a crow.

As close as we ever got was one June, when the Bow was high and over the road and up into our front yard. Magpies were nesting in the spruce trees, we knew, and we wandered down to look at them, more to test our rubber boots than anything else, when we came across the bedraggled baby magpie who had picked the wrong time for his first flight. Flopping in the murky cold water, he would have drowned except for his rescue. His parents weren't in the least grateful, and they dive-bombed us all the way back to the house.

Dried off, and sitting in a box by the fire, the little black and white exclamation point of a birdling was so grateful himself he wouldn't let any of us get within three feet of him. The reptilian hissings and anxious flutterings he made let us know that birds are more closely related to the Komodo monsters than they are to us. Our attempts to keep him alive by eyedropper failed, principally because we couldn't keep him still long enough to feed him. We wouldn't have known how – or dared – to split his tongue.

The ravens speak so well their tongues would never need to be cut. Along the alleys they stand on the tops of the telephone poles. (They know they could never trust their weight to the lines.) And they speak in such a splendid cluster of consonants they put to shame the McCuskers of this world who would prefer language to be simple-minded. A rivulet of chuckles, a stream of profanity, a gusher of consideration, a spate of wrath, a subsiding murmur of content – all of these things I have heard from the ravens.

Perhaps you can understand why I miss them. Winter is a time of reduction. Sounds, odours, colours, tones and distinctions are diminished. There will be a grey this winter as there is each winter, when the sky, the snow, and even the trees and faces are grey. That will be the day when the pure blackness of the raven will be needed, to exclaim the lost light and proclaim the language that is his alone and to share.

8 JANUARY 1975

Winter has drawn silence about itself like a sleigh robe.

The air is crystalline, ice-fogged and sun-dogged, and I hear, breaking like static from a super heterodyne, the music of the skating rink. Strauss, Waldteufel, Tchaikovsky and Victor Herbert live in the woods on the other side of the river. Orchestras dwell in the tall spruces.

At two o'clock the music began and it continued to six, and then an hour and a half of silence. From seven thirty to ten it continued; then the violinists put away their instruments, and Johann and the rest put down their batons and the nether shore was reclaimed by the coyotes.

The path from the schools to the rink led through our yard and the Simpsons' and the Lefroys' to the float bridge at the end of Buffalo Street. It crossed the Bow to the trees and the Christmas tree lights, and through a well-worn hall and into that world of perennial waltzes, Waldteufel, and pom pom pullaway.

Skating was at the very beginning a long and terrifying journey about the perimeter of the ice, holding on to the boards, step by slippery step – red line, blue line, red line, goal line, half way, and falling, sitting and attempting to get back up, struggle, struggle, fall.

Skating was Mr. Paris who was there every day. And it was Mrs. Simpson from four to six teaching the girls to figure skate. And Mrs. Simpson trying to keep the boys out of the way while spins and whirls and eights were being practised.

Skating was races and tag and trying out speed skates. It was seeing how fast you could skate backwards, collisions, disasters and bleeding noses. Crack the whip.

Skating was snow on the hot iron stove in the changing room. Spatter, sizzle and dance, and blow on the dancing drops of water to see how long they will last. Charred mitts that sat too long on the edge of the stove to dry them out. It was the trek through the snow to the drinking fountain, a snow queen's castle of glassy ice, and a tin cup on a chain which had to be broken from the ice.

It was ganging up on another guy and attempting to throw him into the girls' changing room.

It was the beginning of romance. Skating hand in hand and consummating the affair with a not very secret kiss in the penalty box. (Strange symbolism there.)

It was gliding forward with your eyes to the air and watching the snow appear in the cones of the floodlights and trying to catch the flakes on your tongue.

The walk home in the darkness, and watching the moon rise, and spotting Orion or looking for the Big Dipper were part of it too.

And the music never stopped.

It was a shock when I discovered one day that the music we heard was not strictly that of the skaters' world.

After one has skated outdoors amid the falling snow it is not easy to accept the idea of skating indoors.

I haven't skated since the rink came down.

15 JANUARY 1975

Ike Mills' Riding School was located right across the street from us, a paradise any kid would wish never to leave.

Cowboyed, manured, cuspidored, chickened by Alma's chickens, smelling of leather, sweat, oats, hay and horses, the stables were just a little bit mysterious, romantic, out of joint, suggesting danger, adventure, something both kidlike and very unkidlike.

Ike's dogs were mostly gone by the time I appeared on the scene except for one or two that were around the place, and the threat of their being vicious was always suggested by Ike, though I can't recall any of those dogs ever biting anyone. The horses themselves were a threat, too, for though no one ever got kicked it was a possibility; and when the horses were being saddled up it was a narrow path to walk between them from Bear Street to the back of Noble's store and safety.

Alma was a gracious lady, and from the time I was three I cannot remember not being welcome. My brightest memory is being offered a glass of beer when I was about five, a small glass of beer, and no beer since has been such a sweet combination of tingle and bite. Usually, however, it was ginger ale and cookies. Whether there was more magic in the small confines of the overwarm kitchen of their house or in the dark caves of the stables I cannot tell.

The manure box was the greatest danger of the place. Probably no kid who hung around the place, and there were many of us, managed to avoid being tipped into the warm stench of the deep box by Ike or one of the cowboys, and I can't recall its keeping any of us away. My cousin Peter when he was about six or seven went over to show Ike and Alma his brand new Sunday best and ended up in the box, and he feels it was just what he deserved.

Peter's story of his coming back to Banff with his bride typifies best what we prefer to remember about Ike. Peter drove into the stable yard and Ike sauntered over. Before Ike could say anything Peter said, "Is it alright to park here while we go over town?"

Ike let out with a string of curses capable of being heard to the top of Tunnel.

Peter said, "You don't recognize me, do you?"

Ike squinted and looked at him again, probably hadn't seen Peter for a dozen years, and said no.

"It's Pete White."

Ike looked again, really carefully.

"Then," recounts Peter's wife, "tears the size of cow turds rolled down his cheeks."

The stable is gone now, as is the house with its carefully tended garden, and the chair where Alma sat in the hot sun of summer, and the loft and the feed and the halters and reins and the manure box.

But in the golden memories of a hundred kids their true education began in the dust where horses and dogs and Ike and Alma shared everything with them.

2 JUNE 1975

I noticed him Friday, just before I was about to draw a bath, sitting on the edge of the drain, about a half inch away from the focus of the anticipated deluge.

I am familiar with people who have bees in their bonnets, people who stir up hornet's nests at public meetings and the wasp sensibility; the hive of activity is known, as is the anthill of industry, and likewise "a flea in her ear."

But what, pray, does one do with a bee in one's bathtub?

Big, fuzzy, black and yellow, a singular, solitary menace to peace of mind and the next best thing to godliness, he (and we'll let this bee be masculine, though who can tell about bees?) circled the plughole and then took a short walk up toward the midtub section before he turned around.

We all know how to handle bats in the house by the old flashlight trick. When ants get in, it's time to call for the man in the silent truck, but that would seem absurd for a singular bee, wouldn't it.

How did he get in, I wondered, where there was no crevice, slot or splinter large enough to accommodate a bee, and such a large bee.

It turned into a waiting game, but he had the edge. Even if he were to evacuate the bathtub he might still be about in the bathroom, dagger at the ready and about to puncture a tender tootsie as the foot came down upon the bathmat after the bath, so the balneology had to be foregone at least until I knew where he was.

Bees by themselves among clover possess no great threat to me. Among the caraganas of July I think they are almost as delightful as hummingbirds.

Creatures undeserving of the noxious vapours of the insecticide can were never more undeserving than bees, and I can only suppose he was as ill at ease in my tub as I was with him about in the bathroom.

I wasn't prepared to take the big step of wadding him into a napkin and throwing him out the door. What is it about us who are prepared to walk a dozen miles of grizzly country who cannot face up to a thumb-sized ball of banded fuzz?

An attempt to drown him I knew would only irritate his anger.

Glorious images of beekeepers covered with a beardful of bees swarmed in my head, and I thought how easy it would be to let him crawl onto my hand and walk him to the lilacs and his industry, if only I could find the nerve.

I became more childlike in my inventions. A trap of a matchbox to snap upon him, a mesh net shaped like a lobster trap, but always the problem of how to get him out of the trap?

Casually in the lucidity of one going mad I let drop a turkish towel into the tub, and hoped he would walk upon it. Then I could snaffle him into it all and carry him to the yard and freedom.

Casually, with the clarity of a dog looking for a comfortable place to lie down, he sauntered to the edge of the towel.

But he wouldn't move to the center where he might be gathered in.

And equally casually he sauntered back to the bottom of the tub after a rest on the towel.

He's still there.

Does anyone have any suggestions?

9 JULY 1975

The nature of the poker game that is played at the Halfway Hut was a mystery to Ray Legace. The players, it's suspected, include the ghosts of Paley, the Daem brothers, and Herman Gadner, and whether an outsider can easily join that elite group is not known.

Ray was a great respecter of the mysteries of the Ptarmigan Valley and took great pleasure in talking about them. The Ptarmigan is a mysterious place, and Ray loved it.

He was a packer and outfitter of the old style.

In 1919 Ray was selected to be the packer for L.S. Amery on a trip to the mountain which later bore the Englishman's name.

Ray took the money which was supposed to buy the grub for the trip, and blasted out on one of the greatest weeks anyone has ever spent in Canmore. And all the money was spent when Amery arrived.

Three days went by in which Ray worked to scare up the money to provide the grub, while Amery sat and waited in his room at the Chateau Lake Louise.

On the fourth day, Ray appeared at Amery's door. "My good man, do you realize you've kept me waiting here three days? I have spent more than a year in preparation for this trip, and ..." so on and so on.

When he had finished his speech, Amery glowered at Ray.

"Jeethuth Chritht," said Ray. "If you'd arrived today, Lord Amery, you wouldn't have had to wait three dayth."

Unarguable in its validity, lovable in its expression – it is a story which seems essentially Ray in its pointedness.

What we also remember is that Ray, while he could say that to Amery, was also capable of regarding all of his clients as "pilgrims," and that he regarded the mountains as a holy land to which those pilgrims came.

I recall Ray talking about the medicine chests they used to take out in the old days. They contained two panaceas, prunes and cheese. "Pruneth if you weren't working too well, the cheethe if you were." The romantic past of the packers is frequently simple and direct. It had to be if the pilgrims were going to stay alive a hundred miles and four or five days travel from the nearest settlement.

Now the voice with its famous lisp is gone and the promise of tales about Three Fingered Pete and other packers will have to wait for the Halfway Historical Society to meet beneath Redoubt.

Ray Bagley once wrote that "Memory rides a quiet horse with a gentle hand on the rein," which is where I am right now, nine years old and staying at Temple Lodge in the golden autumn of soft larches and having a horse saddled up for me to ride up the valley toward Boulder Pass and Deception, riding a quiet horse.

Ray Legace and Alpha were running Temple those days, and in my memory it is the most beautiful place I've ever been.

Perhaps it was then that I became a pilgrim too, though it took me quite a while to come back to the Rockies and see them as I saw them that first time.

Ray's stories of Halfway came later, and they provided a measure of meaning for the place I knew I could find nowhere else.

He was a great respecter, and I think I learned a great deal about respect from him.

I hope they'll allow him into the game on occasion.

He deserves it.

16 JULY 1975

What better to do on a holiday weekend than retreat from Banff completely and visit a lookout?

By the end of a summer spent in solitude among eagles, ground squirrels, dwarf larkspur, marmots, bluebirds, clouds, static on the radio, and stars brushing the shoulder, the lookout people become a little crazy and a little enlightened.

By whose standards? By the standards of those who do not become lookout people, of course.

First off, the scale of the lookout diminishes. A person becomes an eye. Other people become voices. Sheep and golden mantles become friends. A day spent on top of the clouds with other peaks for company results in disembodiment.

Drama is justly made out of the small things: a group of ewes circling a lamb to defend it from the marauding claws of a golden eagle, the special cry of a pika when a hawk passes over, the building of a moon-watching cairn during the few hot or warm evenings of July, the phases of flower colour as the season shifts each week.

In the Alberta forests, life on a mountain top is comfortable. A generator provides electricity for television; the stove and refrigerator are propane powered; the department provides portable showers which use little water; food and other supplies are helicoptered in every three or four weeks. The valleys and the plains are distant. What news of the world that comes in on AM is almost imaginary.

A strange relationship, as yet unexplored, exists between artists and lookouts in Alberta.

Though my list is not complete, it seems that nearly all contemporary artists who have an Alberta connection have at one time or another been lookouts. Harry Savage, ManWoman, Iain Baxter, Sylvain Voyer is a partial list.

It may have something to do with the observation that a lookout for a summer becomes an eye.

Our first day was middling warm, just right for the five mile ascent to the outpost. In the evening the wind came up and the tower was enveloped in cloud or fog or mist. The wind howled in the chimney pipes, and long cones of light extended from the windows into the chalky night. Snow fell during the night, encasing the buildings in stippled surfaces.

The next day was mostly cloudy, though it broke in the afternoon and it was possible to look out to the prairies and Rocky Mountain House to the east, to look west to the foothills near the Ram River where David Thompson got lost during one of his first excursions to find a way through the Rockies to the Pacific slope, to the south where Martin Nordegg and Jimmy Simpson found their route north to the coal basins of the North Saskatchewan.

The last day was clear. The clouds had vanished during the night, and the splendour of stars in the moments before the post-midnight rising of the moon was great. Even in Banff we find ourselves isolated from the glories of the clear night sky, and it was a good reminder that the universe was, indeed, still there.

And so refreshed, enlightened, and a little crazy, we descended too soon.

3 SEPTEMBER 1975

I cannot remember when I became a student of the natural silences.

It wasn't a part of our curriculum, except in grade one when Miss Pogue had us put our heads down on the desk for a minute or so after recess.

In grade nine, I believe it was during the afternoon classes of Mr. Fisk, I spent many wonderful minutes contemplating Mount Norquay, particularly the bold blazon of aspens in the Gulley.

(It was during one of those idylls I was trapped. Mr. Fisk then, as probably now, had the talent of asking his questions first and then pointing them to a specific person. Good pedagogy, but diabolical certainly. I don't know yet what the question was, but it was aimed arrow-like at me. I answered in the chaos of that moment with a substantial "yes," and the rest of the class tittered. "Yes, what?" inquired Fisk. "Yes, certainly," I said. Laughter. "Uhuh," said Fisk, "I thought so." I thought I had fifty percent odds with my "yes," but the question was probably on the order of "Who can tell me the differences between first and third class levers?")

By then I had become a student, as I say, of the natural silences.

With caution and consideration through that beautiful autumn, during the classes of both Mr. Fisk and Miss Chapman, I watched the gradual changes from the waxy green to the first pale effusions of yellow, the brightening of the yellow towards gold and brilliance, watched the deepening of the sky from the pale cirrus-lightened blue to the deep cerulean of September's finest days.

There is something very fine about sitting in a classroom and letting your mind wander out of doors where it more probably desires to saunter.

On Saturday last, a fine and winding day, I sauntered to the Fenland Trail, and listened to the music of the place. Silence danced in the spaces of that place. Among the spruces, squirrels were busy, magpies were engaged in that file-sharpening business of theirs, and by the bands of the stream soft rustling rivulets wimpled the surface.

I walked the trail in counter-clockwise style, at odds with the instructions of the designer. Principally I wanted to see how many people were there besides me, and there were but two others, both of them townfolk interestingly.

The last fleabane are still blooming. Mushrooms abound. Silence moves with dragonflies. And the woods seem deeper in the near equinoctial daylight.

Nothing happened. Nothing had to happen.

It took an hour to walk a mile because so much was happening, small plants burgeoning in a rotting stump, sweet odours wafting from the squirrel middens. It all seemed ripe and rich.

It is commendable to us all that we can be students of the natural silences, and try to distinguish, as Wallace Stevens says, the difference between the nothing that is not there and the nothing that is.

10 SEPTEMBER 1975

Beavers and squirrels have in common a tendency to overstock for the winter. Each year in October along the Willow River (a commonplace name, yes, but a lovely one, and one that seems to have disappeared from local use), below the railroad crossing, it's possible to see vast stocks of food the beavers have stored. For several years I thought it was an attempt of the beaver to flood out the CPR as their kin have attempted along the Trans-Canada between Forty Mile and the Norquay Junction. But no, it's not engineering they're engaged in; it's lardering.

Spring, summer and fall one sees the great heaps of cones and discarded bracts the squirrels have piled in the woods. And not so many days ago, I was walking beneath a spruce when a great shower of cones rained down upon me. The squirrel at work must have felled more than a hundred cones in a minute. The top of the tree was bare within a half hour.

The cleverest squirrels I can recall used to have two homes. During the summer they lived in the splendour of the Peyto Cabin among the spruces next to our house. The summer they spent in teasing our dogs. Never too far from a tree, they'd venture ten or twelve feet out on to the lawn, getting back to their sanctuary just in time. Then they'd sit and make that strange wheezing sound that is so like a child's squeeze toy. The Peyto Cabin was undoubtedly just the right temperature.

Come the autumn and by frond of tree bough, tree to tree, bounding, bouncing and springing all the shortened day, they were in circuit, from the Peyto Cabin to the Stage Coach Cabin (now called the Sinclair Cabin), along past the tunnels and the swings, a great looping 180 degrees around our house, almost always visible to us from the kitchen window, until they went out of sight.

It took a while to figure out what was up. With winter knocking at the door, the squirrels knew what to expect. They were moving from the cool, temperate summer house to the warmth of the Simpson's house, next door, to a small and cozy apartment right in by the chimney. They were taking their effects with them.

We didn't tell the Simpson's, of course. It wouldn't be fair to the squirrels who had done such a splendid job of finding winter quarters.

Last spring I was standing on Wolf Street, talking to Jim Santa Lucia, who pointed out to me in the pleasant spring day the squirrels who were living in Gus and Vasso Baracos' attic. He hadn't seen them for the coldest spell, but come that warm day, the squirrels were out and sunning themselves and stretching their muscles. I don't know if they've moved in for the fall or not, but I mentioned it to Gus, and he didn't seem particularly perturbed by the information. Guess he figures squirrels deserve a bit of comfort too.

15 OCTOBER 1975

In our family Skoki has a mythical reality which makes it far more important than mere fact. Every family has its myth; I intend only a particularization here, not any claim. One family I know had for its own myth a "land where lost things go" – the other sock, the mitten that went astray from its "idiot string," the drawings their daughter did when she was three that were going to be part of her heritage, the dreams they had when they were twenty-two, the kitten that disappeared three weeks after it came into their home – a poignant, and for them, a rewarding myth. Others I know revere Never-never-land, the Land of Cockaigne, the Verbal Universe: your myth is your own.

But out there, beyond Deception and Redoubt, is the land and the place that has had only a mythical reality for me since I was about four, where Harold and Bubby used to go for a week and come back suffused by an inner glow, tanned and vital and supremely happy.

We went this past week to Skoki, Catharine and Cliff and Peter and I, for three days of memory and quickness, exercise and myth-seeking. Cliff was there a year ago, Peter was there thirty years ago, we're not sure when Catharine was last there, and, shame, I had never been there.

Peter wondered why he had been away so long from what had been his backyard when he was a kid, and has vowed to return in the summer, too. Catharine was gleeful at seeing the log in the lodge on which was written "peeled by Mrs. Peter Whyte, October 6, 1930". (She hadn't written it; one of the builders had put the inscription on with pencil and the varnish has preserved it.) It's the only graffito in the building. Most of one morning was spent in reading the old guest registers, reading the lines and in between them. Romances, it seems, were frequently sealed with a trip to Skoki. (No, you don't have to go to Skoki to read the guest books; the originals are in the Archives, the lodge has copies. Yet there is something in reading the books in their place which is important.) Each page suggested a story.

Three days and three types of weather. A flat overcast with strong winds across Ptarmigan Lake the first day, dry falling snow the second with a return to the lodge in nigh-whiteout conditions, and the third and last day paradisal and powdery, an easy hour on the summit Deception, just lazing around, watching Cliff do telemarks, and sitting there just a bit too long, for the snow was heavy and thick by the time we got to descending, sunburned and revitalized.

We walked slowly that last day, avalanches booming around us from the towers of Pika and Ptarmigan, our track broken for us by four employees from the Chateau, so the way was easy. It was a lingeringly beautiful, bright day, and there was no need for rush whatsoever.

In spite of the foundation logs which have collapsed in some places, in spite of the second day – which made the third so delightful – and in spite of the imaginary fire we sat in front of for an hour, it was everything it was hoped to be.

After our return we went back to the photographs of Skoki made in the 30s for a bit of archaeology, and came up with more mysteries than we resolved: why were the log columns and supports removed from the interior of the lodge? When was the electrical system taken out? Who built the fireplace? Why isn't there a record of the placenames or nicknames which were given to the slopes in the 30s? Bunker Hill? Mount Carson?

The myth and the reality, however, became one for the magical three days of the journey.

7 APRIL 1976

Norman apparently was discovered by a visitor to the Luxton Museum just about a year ago. She was looking at the exhibits, perhaps in the area of the burrowing owl, and noticed a small, furry and quite cute rodent. Bending to take a closer look, she was startled when the exhibit fell from its haunches and scurried away around the corner and, I suppose, into a crack in the wall. Norman had been discovered.

Norman is a golden-mantled ground squirrel of the "cute" variety. Throughout last summer he learned in the typical "cute" fashion to become a considerable beggar and storer of foodstuffs. Various visitors to the town were known to have gone to the museum just to see Norman. In short order he became one of the most famous animals in town.

Attempts to trap and remove Norman from the museum all failed. Norman was removed several times and as frequently reappeared. September came and Norman was seen less frequently. His naps were obviously growing longer. By the end of October Norman was not to be seen at all.

Would Norman reappear in the spring? The staff at the museum had come to love their little resident exhibit, and in the growing days of March it was hoped Norman would reappear. On schedule in April Norman emerged, none the worse for his long snoozy winter, ready to snaffle and store fresh troves of peanuts.

Imminent doom, a cloud of gloomy foreboding, hung over the museum. Each year the Luxton is fumigated with cyanide gas. The museum is sealed up and the gas is poured in. Then the museum remains sealed for a week and the gas does what it is supposed to do, kill the insects, silverfish, vermin, and ... I suppose, stray and passing rodents including golden-mantled ground squirrels.

Norman would have to be live trapped before the fumigators arrived. A week of enticement and appealing lures set out. Norman wouldn't take the bait. Each day for three or four days the trap sat out and Norman wouldn't go near it.

Finally the day of doom arrived. Norman had not been trapped. The fumigating hoses were set up, and the deadly vapours were exhaled into the museum.

Silent and sombre faces watched the operation.

Then the doors were sealed and Norman was left to fate.

For seven long days the doors of the museum remained sealed. The deadly gas was doing its work, exterminating larvae and fungi and rodentia.

Finally the doors were opened and the staff of the museum entered.

Silence met them. The museum seemed unusually still. (Even museums have some moments that are more still than others, ungrammatical as that may seem.)

Ceremony seemed in order for the small friend who had chosen, it would seem, the freedom of the museum rather than the terrors of the trap.

A baleful face opened the door to the staff area of the museum.

And there, sitting up, hands out, perky and prim, Norman stood.

Their anxiety at an end concerning the fate of Norman, the Luxton staff had been handed a new dilemma. Should they refuse to pay for the fumigation which had so obviously been unsuccessful?

I do not know that it was an actual dilemma, but it would have occurred to me.

Norman is happily back at his appointed rounds again. Posing as an exhibit, frightening tourist ladies, seeking handouts, all the usual things a museum squirrel does.

Who named him you ask?

That, my friend, is a darker mystery than how Norman survived, but may be tied up in the nature of his survival. Who knows?

9 JUNE 1976

Elsewhere in the paper appears a short article on Temple Lodge, which describes it as an anachronism, which in part it was.

Now it becomes a monument of memories. My memories are not as acute as those of my cousin Peter who thought of Temple as his first and major home in the Rockies. He will take its burning hard, I imagine.

Temple, for me, because I first visited it in autumn, was a place of larches and clarity and quietness. That was back in the very early fifties and the lodge was being managed by the Legaces then. We were there for three days, and my major memory isn't even associated with the lodge. We were coming by horseback from a ride to the Baker Lake area and I had become separated from the three others in our party. My horse had balked in the woods by Corral Creek, and I had to get down off the horse and into ten inches of gumbo in order to lead the horse the two or three hundred feet to the corral. The incident has coloured my attitudes to horses ever since.

The other vivid memory is of going up the trail to the prospect of the Bow Valley. I had a dachshund with me then as now, and somehow I was sure that cougars, grizzlies, wolverine or eagles were going to startle us, scoop up the dog and be gone. Yet that short trail through the drying stalks of columbine, the soft squash of false hellebore after frost, was the very first memory I have of what it felt like to be on a mountain trail – and it was fresh, cool, and splendid. No cougar spoiled our day.

I never knew the lodge in its in-between, its days as residence for lift staff.

It was winter, twenty-five years later, I came to know the lodge again. Its tone was not so different from the days of the fifties. This time I was on skis, and there were certainly a lot more people around.

Memorabilia on the wall, photographs of the old days, trophies of now ancient races, the lodge seemed to sum up everything that skiing in the Rockies ought to be. A day of good exercise, followed by the possibility of a hot shower and good conversation by a crackling fire in intimate circumstances. Temple had a glorious scale to it. Neither too large nor too small. Just right.

Temple was one of those very few places that had magic.

Temple was one of those very few buildings which had character.

It seems like the loss of an old friend.

Cyril Paris said, when I had told him Temple had burned, "One of the worst things I recall is the burning of our first lodge up on Norquay. We sat down here in the town and all we could do was watch it. There was nothing we could do. There was no way to get there. All we could do was watch it."

It must have felt the same.

The fragile past of our history is always just a spark or two away from burning down.

Temple's last days were beautiful ones. It had its rosy warmth again, its cosiness, its crackle and its story.

It was a hearth surrounded by warmth.

It was and is a model for what a lodge ought to be.

16 JUNE 1976

You have probably run into the "you remind me of..." phenomenon as frequently as I have. It's amusing, and I shan't bore you with the comparisons or likenesses I've heard, except to say that you should be as amused by my likeness to Frank Mahovlich as I was.

The phenomenon has been explained to me recently and reasonably. People wandering among strange faces are attempting to come to some sense of order, trying to find anything that will be familiar and will link on to the merest fancied resemblance in trying to find a way out of their chaos.

I wouldn't have made so much of the comment if it had not been for a conversation I had with Dennis Burton, a quite well known painter who was in Banff for the month of June. Dennis asked me if I had ever seen faces in the mountains.

I was raised attempting to see the Duke of Wellington in Pilot Mountain and always failing. Trips up the river on the *Arrow* or the *Swallow* with my Uncle Allan always involved another scan of Pilot, sometimes to see the Duke, sometimes to see the "pilot," always failing. I can see the Indian chief in full regalia in Mount Rundle. That's not very hard. A friend ruined Mount Hector for me by pointing out that it's a big bunny rabbit followed by a little bunny rabbit, and now I can't look at Hector without seeing them.

So I told Dennis that yes, I had seen some faces in the mountains.

Dennis went on to elaborate the various faces that had been spotted by himself and other artists in Cascade Mountain.

You wouldn't believe them. Dennis can see the Pink Panther gleefully smiling at Inglismaldie. It was actually spotted by Graham Coughtry. Dennis sees an Arab sheik with his head band on, and he can also see a USAF captain.

Maybe Cascade is just a little too familiar to me, but I really had to struggle to see them. (A little hint on the Pink Panther: he's formed in the snow patches at the top of the central gully of the mountain, and he's quite a bit easier to see in early June than mid-summer.)

Dennis had drawings of the mountain faces which picked them out more discretely, which makes the task quite a bit easier. He said that it's really a help in trying to come to terms with the shapes in the mountain. Find the familiarity in the face and everything else falls into place.

Perhaps the most interesting of the observations, and a keen insight into the way some artists look at things, was the perception by Coughtry of Dennis' face upside down in Cascade. Goodness knows why Graham was standing on his head looking at Cascade.

Some of you will recall the paintings of Cascade which were done by Will Townsend. Will saw Cascade (which mountain he indicated he loathed) as a group of overlaid squares, reducing it to a neat geometry of classical proportions on top of the crescents of the shoulders.

Fairly obviously Cascade is a mountain of more complexity than most of us have thought.

I think of Cascade as a false-front mountain, but that's because of my trips to the amphitheatre. It's a false-front mountain made of scree, which is even more amazing. But only those of us foolish enough to ascend the beast know how rotten it is.

But the point about looking for the familiar in the unfamiliar holds true.

Long acquaintance with the mountain leads us to take it for granted. There's good value in looking at it as a stranger, trying to look at it with naked eyes.

14 JULY 1976

Norman, you may remember, is the golden-mantled ground squirrel who moved into the Luxton Museum in the summer of 1975. Norman, you may recall, somehow survived the dread asphyxiators who moved into the museum this spring to exterminate vermin.

Norman, you probably do not realize, this past summer became the proud mother of a splendid family of squirrelkins – or mantlings? Various attempts to change Norman's name to a more suitable name for a mother were made; but Norman had been Norman so long, Norman she has remained.

Norman's children got Norman into all sorts of trouble. An attack was made one day upon one of the stuffed owls which stands close inside the front doors of the institution. "Norman! If you're building a nest, just ask for the materials." But it wasn't Norman at all. One of the children.

On another occasion a lady was staring at one of the Indian models dressed in regalia. She stared carefully at the accoutrements, paraphernalia inter alia, and finally her gaze came to meet upon the headband and feathers. "That's not a feather!" she shouted, just as the feather moved. One of the children again, of course, who immediately darted down from the capital position it had taken to better survey the comings and goings of the visitors.

Burrows were found dug in the display exhibit sand. One of the children. Mad comings and goings. Too much begging. Maybe the father, maybe the children. Who could keep track of the comings and goings?

It was becoming too much of a good thing.

It's one thing to have a clean, little, cute little, perky, sweet pocket gopher. It's quite another to have a mad, thrashing hurley burley of squirrels.

Once again the threat of the trap gas posed. One live specimen in a museum might serve to keep things in balance. Five live things tugging at your pant cuffs and cocking their little heads in begging postures and carrying on like Chip and Dale squared is more than the most tolerant of museum personnel can abide.

But Norman, clever little woman that she is, got the situation right under control.

If the children were smart enough to engage in rapscallion, tatterdemalion tugs o' war, let 'em see for themselves the vast world beyond the walls. So, off they were scattered, tossed untimely from their homes, the shelter of the nest, into the glowering skies of July.

And peace settled about the serenity of Norman once again. Luxy, Toney, and Musey are gone now, and not a trace has been seen of them since.

Norman's vanished for the winter now again. She had a good summer of it, pounds and pounds of peanuts she cajoled from the staff she secreted away, nest building materials galore she accepted and bore away into the hidden labyrinths that twist behind and beneath the museum walls.

It has been an age it seems since that first bright day in July 1975 when the great wooden doors of the museum were spread wide for air and Norman entered smiling the halls of the museum, to entertain and enlighten keepers and visitors, adults and children, to demonstrate, as André Malraux argued, that the walls of the museum are truly artificial, that it is all part of the continuum of experience. Norman has been a lesson, and a delight, and has been a great educator.

Long may she live therein!

13 OCTOBER 1976

The magic of November is a secret magic. As the earth strips itself down, and the long nights' frosts endure almost until noon; as the sun falls behind Sulphur just a little earlier each afternoon; as in the morning we rush a little faster, linger more briefly; as the dusk is sooner a richer indigo, we do not sit long outside, or ramble as far, or consider taking a bag lunch along.

The rich rot of the leaves is done. Occasionally a peek of sunlight glazes the seed heads of the clematis, and for a moment the brightness of early autumn is remembered. The sun while it is about is bright, slanted, oblique, shafting our eyes. It is a mystery of reduction.

What happened to the cadmium yellow of October? Where are the festivals of clouds that revelled in September? And why are the clouds now mares' tails, pale wisps of whiteness drawn in a diaphanous veil, or ringing the sun in sundog splendour? The elk are bugling no more; the birds are quiet; squirrels seem more concerned with labour than with their sentinel chatter. Only the coyotes, late at night, on the nether shore of the river, gather their yipping into serenade in response to the diesel claxons.

Melancholy November. November that seeps slowly into the spirit secretly. November of the hushed voices.

We can be lucky that November here does not come in rain. This November, bright as it has been, has been unusual, for usually it is the flat, grey, low, shadowed November we experience. Novembers elsewhere come in rain and weigh the spirit mightily.

People have been remarking recently that the muskrat houses seem unusually high. Signs of a long, hard, deep, mighty cold winter, they say. The muskrats know.

Injecting just a query of persnicketiness, I ponder the possibility that the lakes are just a bit lower than usual, so that we're seeing a bit more of the muskrat house than usual. I have no facts on muskrats myself, but then I suspect that the other observers have just as much information as I do.

I think we would like to believe, all of us, that it may be yet the coldest winter, the deepest snow, the most ferocious blizzard, the mightiest gale. Something in us yearns for an extravagance of nature that at its best will provide us something to talk about when we too are old timers.

Some of us have become old timers already. The winter of 1968-69 was the coldest on record in this century. In 1972-73 we had the greatest amount of snow recorded to fall in one winter. But one can always hope for another record breaker, not to dispel the stories of ancient days (1973, ha!), but to reveal that we are strong and can endure these things.

The greatest amount of snow did not fall in 1973 anyway. Back in 1948 when I stood about three feet eleven, we had a storm when the snow came up to my shoulders, and it's not going to be that deep again in my lifetime.

But it is premature to talk about such things while the darkly embued and tragic brightness of November surrounds us. If there are no saturated colours here; if the pines have blackened again; if the world is becoming chiaroscuro; let us delight in its slow running away.

17 NOVEMBER 1976

All parades began with bagpipes. Then came Mounties. Then came the parade. Parades began things: reigns, Indian days, memorial services on Armistice day, and carnivals (which were never known as winter festivals in those dim days).

Preparations, the mounting of the armature of trees which was to become the palace of ice, each glittering, each unique, began in November; floats were designed in secrecy, built in cloistered garages; toward the end of January the ice blocks for the street sculptures went up on the median; costumes for the masquerade were gathered. The whole town went privately zanie.

Carnival was for kids then, though we were told it was really for adults. Broomball games on the Norquay Motors lot, obstacle snowshoe races, ski-joring, sled-mounted chuckwagon races, a fantastic afternoon of what we then called fancy skating at Mather's rink, ski races, flapjack breakfasts on Banff Avenue, games of chance (one year at Silver City, a tent town mounted on the river close to the Skating Rink bridge, another in the converted for the occasion Rocky Mountain Tours garage), buffalo burgers distributed from a stand on the Texaco lot.

The teachers gave up early. I cannot recall that the days were ever declared holidays by the School Board. I cannot recall that during the five-day festivities, which included at least three school days, that we stayed in school for an entire day. There was no chance that teachers' conventions coincided; the teachers were as keen as we to see what was going on, and would not have given up carnival for teachers' conventions. Teachers had their priorities too, and it secretly pleased us that theirs were the same as ours.

The glimpses I have of it now seem undistorted. There goes Alec Forbes dressed up in Harry Lauder togs, hobbling on a beautifully bent briar cane. There's Dave Spence in a red toque handing out stubby brooms for a melee, a free-for-all brouhaha, broo-ha-hahmball game. There dash the queens on snowshoes for the first time in their lives, stumbling into deep snow. Here we are gathered on the steps of the Cascade Ballroom watching those wild, costumed people entering the place we could not go, a couple dressed as gas pumps, a woman as Carmen Miranda, hula dancers, Samurai warriors. (No, I wasn't around when Ike Mills and George Childs went as Mama and Papa Dionne with five local tads as the Quints, the night that Ike continually wound up his purse, loaded with rocks, and brought it down upon George's bowler driving it down on his bridge, but I feel as though I might have been there.)

There go sleigh rides up to the Cave and Basin and back, where we spent as much time running behind the sleigh as we did riding on it, and there goes the man who stole the rattlesnake meat from Jenkins' groceteria (and that mystery kept the town gossiping for an entire winter), here is the seal carved by Jim Davies that won the ice sculpture contest balancing its ball on its nose, and here lie the pieces of Nicky de Grandmaison's which he smashed when he didn't win. (It was a goat; and we all thought it should have won.)

The whole town was part of it then, from toddlers who couldn't stand up on skates all dressed up in finery by Mrs. McCullough, Mrs. Simpson, and Mrs. McBride, to anyone who could watch a parade or a coronation of next year's queen.

Sans television, sans cocktail lounges and their "entertainment," sans sophistication, carnivals worked in a wonderful way and drew us together beautifully. I do not think they can happen again.

9 FEBRUARY 1977

The girl from Ottawa came into the bookstore during the early summer. She wanted to know how to get to Eldon. (Eldon is a siding on the CPR; it used to be better known than it is now.) She'd bought a map while she was still in Ottawa and she and her boyfriend had agreed to meet in Eldon on, say, the 14th of July.

We told her that in all likelihood there wasn't a lot going on in Eldon. "Well," she said, "wouldn't there be a general store there? Something like that?"

"No," we said. "Very likely there isn't even a sectionman's house in Eldon."

"Nothing?"

"Nothing except perhaps a sign on a post."

She whimpered.

Her boyfriend was going to arrive in ten days and was going to meet her at a place they had agreed upon that almost did not exist. Should she sit there for the entire day, out by the railroad tracks, knowing the possibility that he might stand by the road? We suggested she leave notes on various bulletin boards, at the park gate, hang around Banff all day.

"No. You don't understand this guy. If he has to hire a helicopter to get there, he will. Nothing is going to stop him. But there isn't going to be anything there, hey? Why'd they put it on the map then?"

We tried to explain the motives of the map makers, saying that a sectionman had once lived there. We tried to find out her motive for suggesting an assignation in Eldon. She said she and her boyfriend thought Eldon would be a nice small place since they'd never heard of it. Not as commercial as Banff or Lake Louise. Right on.

So we told her where the Eldon flats are, she bought a larger detail map, a couple of other maps, and headed out for the ten days of hiking she was going to undertake anyway.

The day came and we wondered if the two of them were meeting. No helicopters flew over that day, so we assumed he hadn't hired the chopper.

About three weeks later she came back into the bookstore. We were relieved to see her.

"Well, how'd it go? Was he there? Were you there? Was it a long wait?"

"No, nothing like that."

"He didn't show up?"

"I don't know."

"Well, it couldn't have been impossible to find. Did you find the sign at the siding?"

"No."

"There's nothing at Eldon?"

"I didn't get to Eldon."

"Oh, no."

She had gone out hiking as she had planned, she'd met a pile of really nice people, they'd all gone hiking in Jasper for a couple of days, and then the whole group of them had gone off into the wilds of British Columbia for some more hiking, they'd lost all track of time and when the day came she was in Wells Grey Park or the Bowron Lakes or some such place, and she didn't make it back.

We never found out whether the boyfriend got to Eldon or not. She was going to write and tell us, but she never did. If he got there it must have caused some strain on their relationship. But we'll never know for sure.

2 MARCH 1977

An unusual amount of my life is tied up with squirrels. I'm not sure whether it's because squirrels seek me out, or because there is some corner of me that is satisfied by squirrels. There are moments when I anticipate being reincarnated as one, those moments when being a muskox seems just too dour and forlorn an existence.

Those highways in the trees that squirrels develop, their moving from spruce frond to spruce frond in an extra-dimensional freedom seem the realization of exhilaration that few others of our neighbourhood animals seem to attain. Some may think of squirrels as chattering visceral bundles of nerves loosely bound in shrouds of russet elegance, moving and sounding in squeeze-toy erratics, but I think of them as question marks of curiosity, their tails curled into queries above their wide-open eyes, their tails occasionally straightening into exclamation points to punctuate their outbursts. What would the forest be without their points of punctuation?

That there is so much going on in the forest for squirrels to remark upon should open our eyes to the life of the forest. Nothing can move, whiskey jack loud or lynx silent, that escapes the all gathering eyes and ears of squirrels. One would believe, mayhap, that there is no glade of conifers that does not have its family, for as one walks along or wanders, the persistent existence and sounding of the squirrels are counterpoints to the soft squash of footfall on the underbrush. Yet one does not feel he is a stranger because his passing is remarked upon, rather that one is another sentence in the chapter of the squirrel's life.

For forty years or so the bird feeder has hung in the same place, by a wire from the eaves, before the window where the visiting chickadees and nuthatches can be observed, and for forty years the feeder has seemed to be squirrel-proof.

This fall, however, matters changed. By a bold leap from the shutter, arcing through space, miscalculating the distance eight or ten times, picking himself up, brushing himself off and starting all over again, the squirrel finally attained the feeder, its nuts and peanut butter.

The skirmish has led to a polite war, attempts to thwart the boldness of his forays, barriers made of card that would allow the birds to get through but not the squirrel, all of which failed. I have to admit that I didn't want to succeed too early, but the gradual escalation of my attempts only served to educate my opponent who was consequently capable of meeting the next stage with greater ease than had there been a quantum leap in my own imagination and ingenuity.

His persistence finally overcame my contrariness. I have relinquished the battlefield. He can have whatever, however, whenever he wishes.

He knows it, of course, and pique gave way to truce, which has given way to friendship. Now he is coming ever closer, curiosity driving him, and his nervousness idling.

I cannot tell if he regrets the wages of our wits, whether he hoped it would go on to springs, strings, deceptions of false feeders, contraptions, thingamees, thingamgigs, widgets, wobbles, and doodads undreamt of before in skirmishes between man and squirrel, but even without meeting Rube Goldberg wildness there is a super-technocratic squirrel who could meet them, should I decide to throw him new curves. He deserved to win.

16 MARCH 1977

After a leisurely trip to Skoki and a fine meal of lamb, we retired to the sitting area to bask in the flames of the fire, partake of the excessive amounts of booze we had carried in with us, and engage in typical Rocky Mountain conversation. When the staff were free, I took out a copy of the Deegan and Porter *Timberline Tales* and read some of its scintillating verse to the small group of us. The tales of Sam Evans and Ray Legace caused much amusement, as did Deegan's saga of his "Birthday to Remember," and then I turned to John Porter's rhymes about Halfway Hut.

I gave it a chilling, I think, reading, and then gave the copy of the book to the lodge for the delectation of other guests.

From there we went on to talk about ghosts, unexplained events, apparitional matters, ectoplasm. Tristan was much engrossed by it all, and wondered just how accurate these stories are. But she had just gone to bed when the rest of us heard a clatter from the kitchen area. Susan wondered aloud what had happened; none of us were particularly spooked by it. Then she went into the kitchen and came back to report that the platter with the leftovers from the legs of lamb had fallen from the shelf to the floor, that it had not been pushed by the dogs, and that the foil which was covering it had come off. There was no way it could have fallen from the shelf it was on to the floor without spilling the goods, but the goods weren't spilled. We can't really say we were haunted by it.

Tristan was a bit skeptical the next morning, and we didn't have any proof of the matter.

But there are those strange matters at Skoki. A well informed and quite decently sane man from Calgary earlier this year was roused in the middle of the night by the sound of wood being chopped. He inquired in the morning and found no one else had heard it. The hope was expressed aloud that if there were ghosts about chopping they should leave more than ghost kindling.

I wrote a poem about Paley several years ago in which I attempted to balance and use and dispel the ghost stories. So far as the supernatural material was concerned I took Cyril Paris's line, that if there be a ghost in the Ptarmigan he is a benevolent ghost. I bring the matter up for two reasons. Some six or so years ago my dog Brandy (the first time I believe I've ever made material out of my dog) disappeared in the Ptarmigan Valley. I said in wry jest that Paley obviously had been unsettled by the poem I wrote about him and was taking revenge. Brandy, however, made his way over to Skoki and spent an easy night and came back with a party of hikers the following day. Paley, I concluded, had thought the poem quite satisfactory.

This trip I was descending from Deception Pass on the Skoki side when I tumbled and lost a ski. It skittered over the surface while my cousin Peter and I watched it with dismay as it veered toward the deepest part of the valley. Just at the edge of the severe slope it turned over and stuck into the snow, about four feet from the oblivion into which it would have disappeared forever. Brian Patton is inclined to believe that a) the ski was wrenched from the binding by Paley who then b) played a little game with it and me before he let it come safely to rest. Brian believes it, because a skiing companion of his lost a ski on the other side of the pass in something like the same circumstances and it came to rest just as close to the edge of oblivion.

I don't make anything of these events. I just record them for you, and you can make of them what you will.

15 MARCH 1978

The businesss of the river is one of Banff's sustaining pleasures. I suppose I have looked upon the Bow now for thirty or more summers, and have always found it to be among the most pleasing of rivers. The only other river I have spent any time beside is the North Saskatchewan as it passes through Edmonton, a decently powerful river but not as sustainingly pleasant as the Bow.

It used to be that on the portion of the river path between Caribou and Wolf streets there were three places where the path divided into two parts, narrowing down and separating to go on either side of a tree or two trees. It was always our belief that those parts of the path had been designated with bears in mind.

"What would you do if you were walking beside the river and you met a bear?"

"I'd go on one side of the path and the bear would go on the other."

The designers or makers of the trail had that very instance in mind. The bear would walk on one side of the tree – or trees – and we would walk on the other. Path designers are very clever. But in all these years of walking beside the river, even in the days when bears were more common in the town, I cannot recall ever having to test the possibility. Now, of course, there are fewer bears in town, and the small islands of trees are gone from the path so it is impossible to test the foresight of the path's makers.

Since the Bow to me is all rivers, Saskatchewan, Nile, Amur and Lena – all other rivers I judge by the Bow, a tough standard. The Ganges can never be so beautifully green as the Bow; for all rivers must be judged by their greenness, the Bow being so beautifully coloured. The Amur, as we saw it at Khabarovsk, is too wide; a river should not be so wide its other bank seems not to be part of the river.

The Mississippi, which I know only from Minneapolis-St. Paul, is too narrow a river, and does not have forest on its far shore, nor sweepers to increase its graciousness. The Ottawa in flood is too tormented, huge, and dangerous. The South Saskatchewan in Medicine Hat flows between hills that are too soft.

But the Bow at Banff is properly wide, wild, shored, and green, gracious, soft, and swift. It would be difficult to find any other river anywhere which sustains itself so riverly.

I remember a comment passed on to me at second hand, a comment from a Swiss girl who compared our river to hers, and she was much attracted by the sweepers of the river, those trees that lean and incline to the water as the bank on which they live is undercut by the current. "Those trees," she said, "they make the river so Canadian."

Pressed for an explanation, she went on to say that in Europe the rivers are all employed for commerce, and any trees that might grow on their banks must be cut down. A tree could never be allowed to grow out and impede the way of business.

But the business of the Bow is just to flow and be beautiful, and it does its business surpassingly well. It stays the right width, and it turns the right green when the runoff is over and summer is cresting.

It fails to flood with the excess it used to, and we no longer find drowned birds on its shore among the shooting stars, but a few forest fires will get it back to its old violence.

And it continues to be the right and proper place in Banff to get away from the ruck and rattle of Banff Avenue. As one stands on the near shore now, the far shore seems to be the threshold of the wild world. The river restores balance.

25 MAY 1978

Praise to Lawrence Grassi.

A marvellous picture of him hangs in Lake O'Hara Lodge, at his wheelbarrow, looking impatient with the idea of standing still for a photograph, anxious to get back to the work of building the trail.

Was he at work on that supreme example of trail-building, the path to McArthur where yards of gravel had to be transported by wheelbarrow to fill in the crevices between the boulders that he had leaned his weight against to move aside?

Or was he on the path to Oesa, where he made stairs and steps so naturally out of materials at hand that many who pass that way do not stop twice to think that perhaps a large man's strength was necessary to effect those small wonders that ease the way?

I thought about Lawrence again last week because I made my way to Merlin Lake along the path that crosses the great screes of Pika Peak from Skoki to Castilleja Lake. It had not occurred to me before that Pika Peak might be so-named because there were pikas on it. Pikas on it? I have never seen such thriving colonies of conies. Those great fellfields that we crossed for a kilometre or more were home to hundreds of pikas, their piles of hay placed along the way to dry on a not very dry day. (Is the proper collective a "persistence" of pikas? A "gathering" of conies? I think perhaps the latter, but am open to suggestions.) Pika Peak is better named than Ptarmigan Peak, where I have rarely seen ptarmigan.

But Grassi's trail, yes, that is our subject. It had rained that day and it had rained hard, and on all that trail only ten or fifteen feet of it were bogged up by the rain. It rises easily and swiftly to prospects of the Merlin Meadows and the Little Pipestone Valley and Skoki Mountain. It finds its way by miracles of routing through a maze of jumbled boulders, by leaves of sorrel, maple red in the swiftening autumn, past the last grass of Parnassus to the springs that feed

Castilleja. There the trail dwindles and the way is found by following cairns or colophons.

What a wonder it would be were our other trails to be built with the same sense of design and consideration as the Grassi trails. The Grassi trail to Merlin Lake is wonder in itself, but after one had made his way up the overdozed travesty of a trail from Temple to Boulder Pass it is even more sublime. Would there were a Grassi among us who might place a footpath from Temple (the new Temple which is under construction right now) up onto the ridge which leads to the Richardson Bowl (where there is a trail already) and Hidden Lake, thence across the ridges of Ptarmigan Peak to Packers' Pass. It's easy enough to scramble from Hidden Lake to Boulder Pass, but a well-designed trail would open the area up to the less-intrepid, separating the foot traffic from the horse traffic (to the comfort of both groups), revealing a new prospect of Mount Redoubt to many people. (The other advantage would be that views back to the ski area would be limited, causing less rancor between the vista and the idea of what it ought to be.)

There are monuments to Grassi, most of which are his trails. There are the Grassi Lakes above Canmore, the Grassi Ridge on Wiwaxy at O'Hara, the Grassi Lookout on Sulphur (little known and lesser known as the years go by, but still remembered). There is the plaque on the way to Oesa, where his magnificent steps were built.

But the greatest honour which could be paid the man would be for the trail designers and builders of the paths of the Rockies to look at the manner in which he built his paths, and then go forth and do likewise. I can think of a dozen places where his insights might be applied with benefit to both the hiker and the environment.

The Rockies shall not easily wear away what he built. Centuries from now the pilgrims shall make their way to Lake McArthur along his path, and they shall wonder that one among us had so much art and skill. His name by then may be forgotten, but his art shall not.

20 SEPTEMBER 1978

Why is it that I stay up late the evening of the shift back to Standard or Stanford Fleming Time, and thus miss any advantage which might be obtained by luxuriating an extra hour in bed?

And why is it that no matter how frequently I escape Calgary on the western route it is always exciting to come into that confluence of the tunnels of the Kananaskis and Bow valleys?

How does it come to pass that I cannot find the attributions I make to other authors in their books? Is it evasive action which leads me to put my phrases in their books? Where they are not?

There is a pattern in the questions which suggests something autumnal, because there is a pattern in the answers. Inevitability in rhythm, sequence, the washing away of something stern and hard and cold in something clear and almost transparent.

The oblique stridency of light that etches the world is the distinguishing characteristic. Standard time returns, and suddenly the light is untrammeled by the mists of early autumn.

I saw it just the other day, at dusk, the bright vermilion light above Yamnuska. Neither was there murkiness nor muddiness in it: how clear it all was. It is a singular joy, an ecstasy of the mid-autumn which suggests itself in shadow, sharpness, and the quick flare of the snowy owl that danced for a moment in the light of the headlights close to Lac des Arcs; lightness and ominousness.

I may have been wrong about the snow: I doubt that the sun will have the strength now to remove all the skiffs of the town. As though its stamina was dealt a mighty blow by the shift to Standard Time. But the obliqueness and the bleakness which the snow outlines are all the burden of the solstitial decline.

And that I could not find the phrase, have not found it, a line I attributed to Octavio Paz who I said said "poets are a creation of language designed to sustain itself," is also haunting, just a little frightening, and also autumnal, if I stop to think too long about it.

We do not have the time to stop and think of time in the almost endless days of June in all the greening joy of spring becoming summer. When Daylight Time is introduced we take it as an unearned bounty we somehow deserve to have for being part of spring and in this world. The summer solstice slips right by, and when the warmth catches up to the sun, it is an unconsidered inevitability.

But when the cold is gone before the sun is at its lowest and the sun has become the nigh-extinguished squib of John Donne's poem, we have much time and darkness to stop and think of time. Retreat to the book again by Octavio Paz to see if somewhere he might have said what I've attributed to him.

If he did not say it, then he should have. And I can glimpse his source in that other wit who said that animals are a creation of water designed to transport itself from one place to another.

But, while the light is fading from the world and making it all clear, transparent, contrasting more the shade against the brilliance, and we Canadians return to being "the intellectuals of the seasons," and marmots, ground squirrels, and the bears go into their deep sleep wherein they'll dream of us thinking about them, I shall sustain a revelry for all the narrowing gate of daylight in this dark passage of the year.

I've cited it before, the observation of the Scandinavians who say of this obscured season that it is like "entering the tunnel," but it seemed even more clear these last few days. Ay, there's the portal, there's the passage: the way is dark, and we must huddle together lest we become lost from one another. We would have each other's warmth.

Now the light is dying. Come, let us consider time together, time and the cycles of the year.

1 NOVEMBER 1978

I was probably five or so the first time I ever went to visit Ping. The place is still there, deserted, solitary, and to a good proportion of the town forgotten. Just behind the Dominion Cafe, off the alley, back of where the Styles used to live: of course you know the place.

I poked my head in the door a few months back, and it was just as dark as ever, and more lonely for Ping's absence. I noted when I put my head in what I had never noted before, that the building was made of logs, and it's my guess that it's among the oldest buildings in Banff. (Does anyone know its history?) The logs were never visible when I was a child because then they were concealed behind the bolts and hills of bolts and mountains of bolts of cloth: wool and cotton and gabardine. There was so much cloth in there it seemed there couldn't be room for Ping too. But there he was, always at the west-facing window of the small one-room cabin, at his sewing machine, huddled over his task in the half-light of that always warm place.

He always had time to stop and talk with us. Can I remember what we talked about? Well, not particularly. I imagine we gave him the news of being five years old, where we had ventured and what we saw, and how the world was burgeoning forth always with quite wonderful things, and Ping would laugh and smile for us. He was always such a gentleman.

The day eventually came, at six or seven or eight, when we were to make the big step toward adulthood, a step which in Banff was measured by receiving the first pair of Ping-made tapers, the most elegant sort of pant that the world could ever imagine.

One went to Ping's after four one day to be measured. Ping made his notations from the tape measure in some sort of magical script on a piece of paper that never seemed to have a name on it, and we could never imagine how it was that Ping could keep all of his scraps of paper in order. Then we chose the fabric, choosing only the colour, for Ping knew which types of fabric shed the snow best.

And then three or four days later they were ready for final fitting, but Ping's measurements were always so good that there never seemed to be any necessity for further tucks and trimming.

Ping's tapers. What wonderful ski pants. Trim and taut and sleek. They clung like a sheath along the leg and plunged into the ski boot without a wrinkle. Elastic from cuff to cuff held them in place, kept them tight and tapering. One could suddenly strut and move with an easy catlike suavity that had never been known before. In another day they were ready. To be picked up after four in the twilight gathering darkness about the time of the first snow.

Ping's tapers were the style of the town. Everyone wore pants by Ping. Everyone knew what was de rigueur. Ping knew too.

The last time I can recall meeting Ping was about nine years ago. He was walking slowly along Bear Street, going toward the Post Office, I suppose, and we stopped and chatted for a while, but I don't think he remembered who I was. I had changed more since I was five than he had.

Around the corner from the sewing machine was Ping's personal area, a sleeping pallet, a hot plate, and I don't know what else. It was possible when we were five to enter that sacred area, but when one gets older there are areas which are forbidden to the curiosity.

But now all of that is gone. Ping is dead, and the whitewashed building beyond the gate and the small garden is now silent, and our pants are no longer finished by Ping. His best of all possible pants exist no longer.

But while he was here that little room was a place of magic.

22 NOVEMBER 1978

He first appeared in August of 1975. He came in through the great doors of the Luxton Museum, looked up at John Morse who was standing there as a security guard, and proceeded into the half light, blinking and inquisitive.

Since no one knew his name, he was dubbed "Norman". He moved in, unpacked (which was easy, since he had no luggage with him it took no time at all), and became part and heart of the museum.

Norman lived on a complex diet of sunflower seeds, canteloupe seeds, and other such granola snacks as the staff of the Luxton could muster, a rich and diverse diet that far exceeded the caloric intake of less fortunate golden-mantled ground squirrels than he.

In the spring of 76 the staff went through the first of the Norman traumas. The asphyxiators arrived, sealed up the museum, and went away for a week. At the end of the week Norman emerged smiling and tugging at pant legs for a handout. Later that summer Norman disappeared for a while after some antics of stealing grass from exhibits and occasional bits of litter such as Kleenex.

Norman's sex had not been important when he was named. Norman was a lady. Norman in 1976 had a litter of two or three which commenced to raise havoc in the museum, running up and down mannequins, getting into battles with red squirrels. Norman got things under control by banishing her children to a harsher environ than the museum.

At summer's end Norman's visits became fewer and fewer, and at about the onset of October she disappeared. In 1977 a couple of weeks before the asphyxiators were to arrive again Norman reappeared, fresh and antic and lively. The staff again went through the anxiety of trying to decide whether to trap Norman and get her out of the building while the gassing was going on. Norman would not be trapped. Again the building was sealed up, and at week's end Norman reappeared. She had another litter of children that summer, and again at the end of July or so she sent them out into the cruel world.

By 1978 the staff had grown accustomed to the spring shenanigans of Norman, her nesting traits, her capacity to pocket any amount of seeds, peanuts and sundry goodies and retreat with them to her den outside the building. Norman who in her early days had wandered most of the museum was now spending most of her time with the staff in the coffee area, and never ventured out into the exhibit areas. She was genteel and grateful for the lifestyle she had developed.

This spring in April she showed up again, back in the staff area, as happy as ever to reacquaint herself with the staff, still filling up her pockets with food and scurrying away through the secret passages between the walls and out into the yard and down into her den to secret away her troves and treasures.

Again in late April, on schedule, the asphyxiators arrived. Because Norman had passed through the previous three asphyxiations with no particular indication of ill effects, the staff didn't worry too much.

In early May the museum was reopened.

Norman has not been seen since.

It is assumed she is dead.

Members of the staff have inquired of specialists what the life expectancy of golden-mantled ground squirrels is, and it would seem that Norman had lived a full and joyous life. Perhaps in very unusual circumstances a ground squirrel might live eight or so years. Norman at the age of five had fulfilled a longer than normal life, and had brought joy into the lives of many for all her days in and around the museum.

What happened? One of the staff members surmises that Norman, "after all those years of being domesticated, probably changed her abode to under the Luxton Museum itself, and that was all that was needed."

Requiescat in pace, Norman. You shall be well remembered, and your presence will still warm the woodwork of your august home.

13 JUNE 1979

I do not mean to rain on anyone's parade. I saw little of this year's Winter Festival events, and I'm in no position to comment on them. Perhaps I chose to remember what the Winter Carnival had been.

The Carnival was first and foremost the parade and opening ceremonies. It fortunately always fell on a school day which meant that there was more than adequate reason to find one's way out of school. Principals and teachers alike understood the capricious nature of the Carnival Committee, and did not endeavour to keep us in class.

What marvellous parades they were! In memory's eye there were many bands, and floats of a grandeur to pale the Rose Bowl (which in any event we knew only from black and white newsreels), and the main street seemed lined up six deep to ooh and ah at the wit and skill and imagination of the float makers. Now as I recall I can see the phenomenal rocket ship that Brewster Transport assembled. Towering higher than a V-2, it seemed ready to launch itself to the very height of Sulphur Mountain and beyond. The IODE Old Woman Who Lived in a Shoe seemed to crawl like a petrie dish with its hundreds (well, dozens) of kids, involving every member of that organization. It seemed to take an hour to pass, the parade, and was more splendid than the Calgary Stampede's.

Almost immediately afterward there was the assembly at the Ice Palace below the legion. All the autumn the ice had built itself into magnificent shapes of frozen cascades and Snow Queen buttresses, the armature of spruce trees completely hidden beneath the layers of ice. Buffalo robes and honour guards of Wolfcubs and Mounted Police stood by while Mayor Mackay (it seemed always to be Mayor Mackay) extolled the virtues of the splendid midwinter silliness that Carnival was, and talked about the importance of Banff to Calgary, and the crowd which lined the bridge listened politely.

We all looked and criticized the queen candidates; choosing – with no regard for her athletic skills or personality – the prettiest as the one we would have as queen the following year. And then as part of the ceremonies there was a brief display of fancy skating by two of the local girls and a chuckwagon race on ice by the scouts. It all held the aura of specialness.

In the day that followed and the evenings and other days there were buffalo burgers sold from a tent on the Texaco lot, and broomball games at Norquay Motors, ski-joring on the main street behind jeeps or on the river behind horses, curling on the sheet of ice in front of the ice maze in front of the police barracks, novelty races on snowshoes across the barricades and through barrels on Banff Avenue in front of the Elite. There was jumping on the Grizzly Street jump, the masquerade in the Cascade Ballroom, and the afternoon of skating at Mather's rink, hockey games, and such a wonder of festival events and glamour and surprise, it can never be recaptured.

We couldn't go into the Cascade Ballroom, of course, but we could stand outside and watch the costumed masquers enter. I see them now, two people dressed up as service station pumps, a deep sea diver with a mermaid, and, though I never saw it happen, I can also see Ike Mills and George Childs as Papa and Mama Dionne with the quintuplets. (It happened before I was born.)

Tiaras and glitter, royal purple capes and ceremony and fun. Toboggan sliding on Harmon's hill, street dances, and crisp white snow. It was always good weather.

We cannot go back, but memories can be warm.

6 FEBRUARY 1980

We had imagined a "dance of white dragons" and had named it before we ever discovered the place. In similar wise, of course, we had beckoned "Exceptional Pass" to our imaginations long before that place was actually discovered, described and placed on the maps of our mountain minds.

The "Dragons' Dance," as it ought to be more familiarly known, is a brilliantly beautiful place of slithering light that ripples, cascades, coruscates, wavers, wanders and flares with the dazzle that only the imbricated plates of giant white saurians could suggest.

How would you find this place? How would you find dragons? To find yourself in a place of rare magic – wherein dragons most assuredly dwell – you must be in a rare and magical state of mind yourself. Dragons are not casual about revealing themselves to skeptics, and so you must rid yourself of all preconceptions and quibbles. Then you must prepare yourself for a greater immensity than you are used to in the workaday world of mundane normalcy.

Ursula K. LeGuin, one of the better writers of the fantastic real, describes several dragons in her majestic conclusion to the Earthsea Trilogy, *The Farthest Shore*. Until I had read her novel I little realized that dragons are among the hugest caprices of the human spirit. In her story a great sadness occurs in Earthsea when most of the magic of the world is drained away, and it becomes necessary for her hero to make his way to the Western Reach. On the way the small barque sails past a dragon, and in the still days of the mournfully depleted world it takes almost a day for crew to pass the dormant dragon. I had never known it could take so long to pass a dragon, nor that their immensity was so unfathomable.

Earlier – last autumn, in fact – we had seen glimpses of the "Dance of White Dragons" from a ridge to the south of them. Suggestions of the majesty of the monsters were felt as we crested the back of Monstro, but we had little time that autumn day to reverse our steps and proceed back and beyond of where we had come from that morning. But even then we knew it was a place we'd have to visit on a later occasion. We could detect the ring of ice, the glittering summits in which the ring of unknown phantasms swished their tails, in which the overwhelming scale and scope of place would taunt and flout the mere imaginations of us all.

We turned our back upon them then, and made our quick way back to the sheltering valley in the shortened day nigh the equinox, and gave them little thought in the dark dusks of the winter, though occasionally we thought of them , and on the coldest days were wont to think the dragons' grasp was coming nigher.

This weekend past we betook ourselves again to the airy, vaporous realm that lies nearby the "Dragons' Dance." Our consideration on the first eve there, was to wander to the summit of the "Nostrils" only to lengthen our muscles once again for the morrow when we would walk another several leagues to another valley's upper reach, but on our visit to the Nostrils we chanced to trek a fool's furlong up a slope, looked back and over the crest of a ridge and there in the afternoon light the dragons started to stir again in our minds' fancy and the fells of that great valley. Naught else could be for our morrow's journey but that we should climb into their lair.

It was every bit as bright and joyous as we could have imagined it in the greatest expansion of the lackaday world.

Like all the Rockies' boldest, brightest spectacles, the "Dance" gave glimpses of the bright beyond but held its greatest secrets back behind the forest and the way. We surmised beyond the bright lace waterfalls and dappled smithereens of fracturing light we should be adequately rewarded for our efforts, but when we crested the moraine the dragons had pushed up with their bold snouts we were stunned into exalted silence. Eyes could not gather in the panoramic strength and lingering immensity of it all; they blinked against the shimmering size of them, the great turmoil of their past, the desert wastes that lay strewn about in vestiges of violence.

Time is as nothing to dragons. They have danced there for millennia and will dance there for many milliards yet of years to come. Dragons dance in stately sprightliness; and only the movements of our eyes allowed their glancing motions to slip beyond the surly bonds of time and duration to become a moment of the dance.

All of their past and all of their future seemed to come together in a synchronicity of motion, place, and time. Here forelegs fell beyond the cliffs, and here the spume of icy breath began to frost itself in cornice, canyon, scarp and carapace.

20 AUGUST 1980

It's fortunate that these mountains are so rich in passes, if for no other reason than that passes are, to paraphrase John Ruskin, the beginning and the end of all mountain scenery. He who would grow tired of passes would grow tired of the world and its bounties I am sure. I know one person at least who blinks his eyes a little to fuzz them over as he approaches Healy Pass from the Peyto meadows side to make the spectacle of the Egypt side seem more bright, more emphatic than that normally dazzling spectacle is, does it because he wants to burn it in upon his retinas to last a year away from the mountains in Toronto. And yet as he remembers it, it is always less than the actuality of that place, that passage.

When we stop to pause and try to recall the photographs or paintings of passes we recognize the deficiency of visual artists in depicting them. Several years back I stood in London's Tate Gallery before Turner's painting of Hannibal's crossing of the Alps. It is a bold, magnificent painting, mad in mist and snow and elephants. As I stood and looked at it a man and his son came along, and the father talked a little about Hannibal and the story behind the picture, then he turned to me and said, "What do you think?" "That Turner didn't know high mountains very well." "Where are you from," he asked. "Western Canada," I replied. "Ah," said he, "we have no such mountains in England or Wales."

Turner had not seen the Alps yet when he painted Hannibal and derived his picture from Snowdonia if I recall correctly. The mountains are a little softly textured for the Alps, but the painting is, in spite of that shortcoming, a brave, magnificent work. It is, however, and to retain the thread of the argument, one of the few paintings I can recall that handles the concept of a mountain pass with some of the sensations I connect with that type of place.

Part of the sensation of a pass is the effort required to attain it. Part of the sensation is the concealment and the revelation which are so closely enjambed. A pass is not a single point of view, but is a temporal translation. The photograph or the painting cannot disclose what the view was like a moment before the new vista was unveiled. Cinema – which is, of course, like music or poetry, a temporal art – has rarely concerned itself with passes, unless it has been from Cinerama cameras placed in the ball turrets of B-52s. Cinematic technique is not up to the task either, I suppose because the editing of movies too frequently cuts from the scene to another, and a pass would seem much like just another cut.

I found myself in these considerations this weekend past when we were making our slow passage up Wenkchemna. It was a perfect day: mixed muck and occasional scattered sunlight. We turned back once because we thought the clouds were going to settle right in; five minutes later we reversed ourselves again, pass-backwards you might say. "It's a cold and desolate place at the best of times," a member of our group warned, "and on a day like this it's going to be absolutely barren."

A glance back down the valley from which we'd started and we couldn't see a trace of Babel, Fay or Little. "Ah, we might as well go on."

Twice again the mist, the little snow, the boiling clouds embroiled us. As we made our way up the rocky switchbacks, the visibility dropped again to less than thirty metres. Gloves, toques, wind jackets, down vests, and rain gear appeared miraculously from daypacks. From one small cairn to the next we nudged ourselves with little hope. Harsh wind began to blow, stripping away any vestiges of warmth that resided on that slope, and small pockets of snow began to gather on the path.

"We're not going to see a thing," another voice warned. Brief council held, we were so close we might as well proceed further.

We rounded the ridge which bears the trail, higher than the lowest point of the pass, expecting to be hit full in the face again by the wind, staring into the grey and swirling mass of cloud. The deep and swarming caldron of mad weather was hauntingly beautiful.

And, lo, it started to thin. The gathering water of Tokumm Creek beneath us started to be visible. The wild edge of Curtis Peak began to attain some definition and we could see almost to the summit of both Wenkchemna and Neptuak. As we stood there the clouds streamed up and out of the deep vale which was the other side of the pass. Ragged clouds played tag on the ridges of the mountains, and then we could look back and see the meadows we'd traversed, the small amethyst that Eiffel Lake can rarely be.

"We have come to the place where the weather is made," I said, for as we looked again down into the valley of the Eagles' Aerie new mists and cloud were gathering again, and our fifteen minute sojourn in that pass of wonder was completed.

The day had perhaps fifteen minutes of bright wonder and we were there for all of them. A quick glissade down the snow patch and we were back in the dismal soup. The sunlight continued to scatter itself about the day, but we had drunk our fill.

Time had stopped up there, as occasionally it does in mountain places. We had transcended summer, autumn, spring and winter. Yea, it is barren, but it is so beautiful.

3 SEPTEMBER 1980

One of the wise ones, whose name is forgotten, once remarked that there is for each of us a right and proper place in the world, and some of us are fortunate enough to be born into it, whereas others of us have to work very hard to find it. Whether Lizzie Rummel worked hard to find the mountains or not matters little. Once she was here the mountains made good sense for her; and she graced the mountains and made good sense of them.

Ten years ago, I recall, Lizzie called me up because she wanted to know what "oromania" might mean. Five minutes digging in a dictionary and I had learned that *oro* is a Greek root meaning "mountain," and so I reported to her that "oromania" is a high-falutin word for "mountain madness." "We understand this, don't we?" It was her generosity to take us all into the scope of her passion.

Only a person blessed with a smidgin or more of mountain madness could understand and appreciate Lizzie's joy that spring-winter day when she was left alone in the cabin at Sunburst Lake. She had flown in with Al Gaetz to Magog and they had skied up to the cabin; Al had taken the piece of tin off the chimney top, and they had moved her three days' supplies into the cabin, and then he had departed, and in the middle of all that some would call loneliness she was brimming with fulfillment, for she had found the place in the cosmos that was where she was meant to be.

Twenty years later, after a day's trek through the arid elfin splendour of the Valley of the Rocks, a girlfriend and I arrived at Lizzie's Sunburst Camp. We were going to camp in the Magog Lake campground, but Lizzie's was our first port of call. We had a difficult time dissuading Lizzie from giving us dinner right then. Our final argument was that we had packed it up the Valley of the Rocks, and we certainly weren't going to pack it down Bryant Creek. The following morning we dropped back in to see Lizzie and talk to Myrna, and she gave us directions to get to Elizabeth Lake, the tarn a short walk from Sunburst that five Calgary friends named for her. Our idling took us in a different direction. Three hours later we were back to say farewell. Time cannot rust that farewell image of Lizzie waving us goodbye as we started out for Wonder Pass. The previous night we had learned that Lizzie's Sunburst Camp was in its last year of her operation. I had held off not a jot too long. She had come in that summer on the back of a horse. "You should have seen her," Myrna said. "She looked just like a queen."

Lizzie's gusto carried her beyond. She and her sisters attended school in Millarville, and she had a solid foundation in languages from her days in Germany. Even so, I was surprised when in the early 70s she decided to reread Hermann Hesse in English, "just to see why the young people are reading him." That same year she reveled in the delightful paintings of Joe Plaskett's Paris, recalling joyously the days in 1953 when Joe, Jim Willer, and Takao Tanabe had been her guests at Sunburst. All of Lizzie's guests were prizes, and each moment in her fastness by that lake was fulfilling.

I wasn't in Banff in the years that Lizzie lived in the little old curling rink cabin beside the backwater by the boathouse, and when I returned to Banff she had chosen Canmore to build her home in, though she was in Banff often enough with her tape recorder in hand to converse with old timers. (Lizzie and I were talking one day about the remarkable Dorothy Dowhan, and I slipped and said, "How did a person like Mrs. Dowhan end up in ... uh, choose Canmore?" "I heard you," said Lizzie, "you corrected yourself barely in time. 'End up in,' indeed.")

Lizzie made the mountains more magnificent by her presence. By being part of the landscape of Skoki and Sunburst she brought the mountains just close enough to gleam more brightly. She brought a warmth to the lodges that made them snug; and snugness counts for so much more when it is fifteen or twenty miles from the highway. She brought joy into the beauty of the mountains.

Atonement and bliss. She was making her way from Skoki to Temple one spring day, and when she reached the summit of Deception Pass she stopped to survey the grand splendour of Ptarmigan, Redoubt and Fossil, and while she paused on the summit of the col, so silent a whisper could be heard, she became aware of the sound of skis on the snow beside her, yet she knew she had ascended to that point alone, and that no one else could have come up from Ptarmigan Lake. The restless skirring sound of skis. It was Paley, she was certain, who was skiing beside her, just taking care of the skier who travelled by herself.

We should remember the Lizzie always that Jimmy Deegan remembered in his "A Birthday to Remember," the hostess who always threw out the welcome mat. And the Lizzie who, with the help of Myrna, managed to get Arnold Brigden out of his clothes at the "Sunburst Lake Steam Laundry" as he later called it, when he had been camping on Wonder Pass for two or three weeks without a change of clothes. We should remember the Lizzie who always had time for anyone.

If we have a great and glorious past and tradition in these mountains, it is because of generous hearts like Lizzie's, as much as it is for the bravado of the surveyors. For she gave us, what we would ignore at great expense, the warm and very human aspect of the great tradition. She cannot be replaced.

16 OCTOBER 1980

Cyril Paris was for me the standard of what it means to be a Banffite. Born here, loved it here, enjoyed the backcountry fully, explored it, named it (or parts of it) on occasion, thrilled to storm and chinook, was part of the give and take of Banff Avenue, and always had time for a brief chat or a conversation at Post Office or on street corner.

In his quiet, considerate way, Cyril was, and will probably continue to be, a model of what a cultured person in Banff should be. Culture, of course, does not mean that the possessor of it has the fortitude to sit through concerts he does not enjoy, talk about paintings he does not understand, nor does it involve a great deal of reading. Those matters are tied up in snobbery, the caricature of culture and in some ways its enemy.

No, a cultured person in Banff should bring a sense of balance and insight to the particularities of place, have a sense of history, recognize the forces that have played upon this place to make it what it is; Cyril had a judicious sense of balance. Whenever it seemed to me that one particular group was venting a misinterpretation of Banff's past vis-à-vis the government or the ski areas, or recalled some slant I thought too askew I would ask Cyril what he thought, and I would nearly always accept his interpretation of events. Cyril's own modesty, which was solidly related to that sense of balance, meant that he was rarely at the centre of the stories told so well, and if he had not been part of the particular story he would vanish from it. It was years before I realized that Cyril had been one of the first two investors in Skoki Lodge, which was one way of making his belief in skiing into something more substantial than it had been in the formative years. That they decided to invest in a ski-lodge on the verge of the Depression was an unforeseeable accident.

I had forgotten, until I was reminded last evening, that Cyril and some of his contemporaries had been the discoverers of Bourgeau Lake. They had looked up the valley and thought to themselves, "there ought to be a lake up there," and so they had set out to find out for themselves. Getting to Bourgeau Lake whenever that was could not have been nearly so easy as it would be today, for it would involve either proceeding west from Banff along Sundance Creek or crossing the river at Massive and backtracking. It must have been at least a two-day trip. The lake, fortunately, was there for them at the end of a shintangle escapade.

If we look at the three ski areas which now dominate our winter lives, we should recall that Cyril is one way or another associated with the development of each of them, whether it was in clearing the slopes of Norquay ("We were told not to cut down every last tree, and so we left the lone pine," Cyril recalled.), or in developing Skoki which was the start of the Lake Louise Ski Area, or in spending a couple of days at the head of Sunshine Creek in 1929 and recognizing the potential of the place. Downhill skiers notoriously have no sense of history – at least while they are being skiers – but I think that every skier should pause some time this winter and think of Cyril and recognize how much he owes that quiet man who never sought any glory for his contribution. Cyril, of course, did not work alone, but it's my conjecture that the Paris boys and the others who worked so mightily to make winter part of our lives in Banff owed something to George Paris, Cyril's father, who was forever leading the boys of Banff out on snowshoe treks into the woods and forests around the town, up to the top of Sulphur Mountain, or into some tucked away valley. George was not a skier, of course, but he had a love for the outdoors which has come down to all of us.

Culture is a way of living inside the force of myth in the reality of the world. Cyril, I suppose, knew that in those bright days when he and his companions stood on the col of Deception Pass and surveyed the broad white world beneath them they were strangers in a strange land, forever to be haunted by its beauty, to be in the thrall of a gift of nature, that the bounty of the world was meant to be shared. And he took that gift of beauty and dispensed it to others. He had time for the willows and the chickadees, had time to run around the slopes of Temple, had time to talk with strangers on the street.

Cyril would not have stood still very long to be told these things, and would have smiled and turned aside from suggestions that he might have been a symbol of culture. He would have preferred to think of his friend Earle Birney that way. But he was; he most assuredly was.

4 FEBRUARY 1981

Days there are, rare as this summer has made them available to us, that the clover seems to ripen right into our nostrils. All the summer, I had thought, would be rich only with the pitches of conifers, those redolent spruce tones that seem to percolate into the air with each new mistfall or rainstorm, and we would never be able to sustain ourselves with the mellower notes of scent. I've not found rock jasmine yet this summer, and by now it may already be too late for my androsace, but even the clover, lowland plant that it is, is sufficient to reimburse us for those wan, grey days we had too often in July.

If we lived where winter-spring were not so long I'm sure we could develop a full calendar of scents to burgeon in upon us with clarity, but since January smells much like most of March, I fear we'll have to satisfy ourselves with spring's bright clarion scents, the resins and the bursting seams of sap in willows and aspens, the palely cloying thickness of the dandelions, the sweetness of vetch, the penetration of the oleasters on the river bank from their small yellow-grey flowers (which you may know as wolfwillow) that seems to brighten dawn even when the day is overcast in their sharp pungence.

We've had few of those dusty days when the air is still and the pollen seems to hesitate in the air with neither gust nor blast to send it on its way to germination. We've had a surfeit of those mossy, slightly dank, somewhat acidulous days, when each nostril's crinkle seems to suggest a mouldy, liverworstish sort of sensibility. I find a joy, simple but sure, in walking from the roads into the woods upon any trail, and noting that the noxious odours of the highway seem incapable of wafting further than a hundred yards or so; and whether the odours of the woods are boney in the fashion of Miss Havisham's or rich like the moulder of old wood that has been dampened often by the rain, I find an eye-closing revery in the simple sensations that those wafting perfumes of the woods provide.

The other pleasure is in passing from one zone into the next while ascending. We do not need a map to tell us that we've passed from boreal forest into sub-alpine region, for there is a breath of sweet-sourness that seems to come from bracken and from duff that changes instantly when the larch are near. It's never quite so clear in summer as it is in autumn when the pale pink valerian begin to sharpen in the first frosts, and we find our sinuses tighten momentarily as we crest the hill and reach the meadows. It's not a scent that we would dare to package for consumption by macho men or mildewed maidens. (You've noticed I'm sure that among the brands of men's colognes there's one that's called "Timberline." It must have been named by an ad-man who never knew the odour of decaying, bright valerian.)

I've noticed recently I cannot persuade people who do not know the names of flowers to get down on their knees and stick their noses into those beckoning blossoms. I do not know whether it is because I lack the influence I once had, but I find it disturbing. Aileen Harmon used to say – probably still does – that the proper way to approach a flower is in an attitude of veneration: on one's knees. I do know this: that if you wish to know a flower well, she is correct. You must get down to the flower's level, see its blossom's form, inhale its perfume, note its delicacy of colouration, and then proceed further if you wish. I cannot believe I'm hanging around with the wrong sort of people, but it may that television has so removed us from the notions of first-hand experience that we daren't easily accept what nature has to give us so readily and easily.

Meanwhile it's free and easy for us all. This Sunday afternoon I found myself briefly on Banff Avenue before I retreated to the river and its quiet sanity. I shouldn't be so quick to tell so many people that the river is quite so close at hand. But Banff Avenue was aswarm with melancholy looking people, and the river couldn't have been peopled by more than twenty folks or so between Bow Avenue's corners at Buffalo and Wolf. Only one jarring note: I see the old "North Landing" sign is gone. I wonder why. The sign did no one harm. It should have stayed.

12 AUGUST 1981

We stumbled upon Exceptional Pass, almost without expecting it, unaware that it was there until after we thought we had discovered it, and when we got back that way a few years later, as one will insist on going back to a place where wonderful things happened, none of us in our party could remember whether we turned left or right after we went up the final branch of the creek.

We didn't discover it of course. By now it should be clear that the Rockies have been here long enough and the curiosities of their visitors and pilgrims have been strong enough that we rarely discover anything. Caves, I guess, are more likely to conceal their existence from us than a mountain pass is. But Exceptional Pass is, we are discovering, continually being rediscovered, and its joy is that everyone who finds it anew is so taken away by it he thinks it's a discovery. Well, fair warning is fair warning, and the ads have appeared by now so you know it's coming up.

There is something inside the subversiveness of the imagination, the dream-like states where the brain's waves start to construct holographic intersections of ripplings that only discrete light can make roundly and chimerically solid, and the concentrated attention being brought to bear upon a single subject that starts to make it as blithely real as what we normally perceive.

It's strange, but I cannot recall very many psychologists talking about the nature of the imagination. Freud may have gone on to describe the topography of the mind in ego, id, and superego, but he didn't find an imagination. Jung found the anima, the shadow, the archetype of the trickster, and a lot of other figures hovering around the fire of the mandalas in the heart of the psyche, but he failed to find an imagination. Is it something that psychologists really prefer was not there? Jung is willing to describe aspects of the soul, and other ineffable chameleons. Why not the imagination?

A quick conjecture: why not base a psychology upon the concept that imagination is vital to our sense of well-being? Retrace the history of the hominids back to the moment when a cluster of troglodytes were hovering around a small fire of kindling in the back of a cave, away from the wind and the harsh reality of the world, and then recognized that in the cave they were in an evocation of their own condition, and that the hearth they hovered around was the centre of their own sense of mind, that they would otherwise be in darkness but for the small fires in their own minds?

And then further conjecture that it was the first recognition that began to illuminate the path toward evolutionary creativeness?

The suggestion in Arthur C. Clarke's text for *2001* is that it was a glimpse of a new world inside technology that drew humans up from the scrabbling around for subsistence in the dry washes of the deserts and at the edges of the waterhole toward the light of the stars. For his purposes the notion was quite decent, a precept that helped provide a good deal of the majesty of the film. The other aspect of it was Kubrick's concept that beauty is as much of a reward as technology, and so the movie that resulted did wobble magnificently on its two different precepts.

But I think it would be a wonderful science fiction – which is what psychology is in a way, isn't it? – that could develop from looking at the imagination itself.

In a way it is the subject of William Blake in his poems, as it is also the subject of Carlyle's *Sartor Resartus,* and it might be partly what Shakespeare's *The Tempest* is having so much fun around.

I read recently one of the new caveman novels, *Clan of the Cave Bear*. Not particularly distinguished, it lacks the grace of *The Inheritors* by William Golding. But Cavemen and Unicorns are major manifestations of pop culture in the eighties, and we can expect a lot more of both. If we find either group, I wot, it may be by the route of Exceptional Pass.

9 DECEMBER 1981

An amble to Helen Lake and Secretary of State's Ridge last week revealed five score or more marmots, the first of them met with all the delicate rapture one accords encountering "a wild animal in its habitat, shhh!"

The second and third we met with less ecstasy, and by the time we'd met twenty or more of them, all around the trail, digging roots up, basking on rocks, ambling across the meadow, drinking from Helen Creek, little marmots, big marmots, brindled marmots of sunny disposition, matriarch marmots of bland indifference, we began to think we were in marmot heaven.

For all the marmots' scurrying, relaxing, bounding hither to Helen and yon to beyond, the landscape was strangely silent. The Helen Lake marmots are, it would seem, a distinct subspecies: the non-whistling marmot, *le siffleur sans souffle.* From time to time in marmot country I fantasize an orchestra of tuned marmots, banked arrays of bassos and baritones on boulders, tenors on tundra, altitudinous altos and contraltos, sopranos on scree, fluting from fellfield, whistling from willows. I rarely go so far as to believe I might progress along to D'Indy's *Symphony on a French Mountain Air,* assuming in reality it might sound more like those bizarre recordings of the late 50s in which dogs barked out *Jingle Bells.*

But the Helen Lake marmots do not whistle. Should one of those creeps, who likes nothing better than to emit an ear-piercing whistle at the onset of darkness in a theatre, go up there and give them some lessons? Or will the shadow of an eagle falling upon one of them result in some marmot's first declaration? (Sorry, Gordon, I couldn't resist it; maybe you can make something of it.) Who will take on the job? These are marmots who are failing to fulfill their destiny.

It has been pointed out to me that an orchestra of trained marmots would fail, if only because, after one had trained them to respond to the beck of a finger, the first shrill declaration by one of them would cause all the others to shut up. Well, in my marmot heaven they whistle for the joy of whistling.

"Marmots," I elaborated, "would make splendid pets." (No, I'm not suggesting we should remove them from their habitat; I was just getting carried away by the delight of meeting so many marmots on the way.) "Why, if one should decide to take off to Hawaii for the winter, all one would have to do with the pet is put him in the back yard or the rock garden, let him dig down into the earth in September, and when you're back from the islands, you just have to wait until the end of June for him to emerge. During the summer, care would also be minimal. All you need is a home with a dormer. Put him out on the roof, watch him scamper up to the peak of the dormer, and he can sit there all the long sunny days, casually regarding the neighbourhood."

The non-Helen Lake marmot would be the one you would wish for a pet, for the whistling one can also double as a guard-marmot, fifing out alarms at the approach of anything, but really just being happy to gaze out across the vista of roofs, believing them to be mountains. (I read with some interest that peregrines are being introduced into urban environments, for large buildings are roughly equivalent to the cliffsides that falcons choose. Peregrines and marmots could live in some uneasy symbiosis, it would seem, in a penthouse society.)

18 AUGUST 1982

Spring sneaks across the equator so silently we, without our *Old Farmer's Almanacs*, might not be aware of the moment it begins.

Forays of the sun have already hardened by thaw and freeze that snow which its rays have not already diminished. Bursts of light have thrust catkins on the willows. Beside the road near Morley a week ago ground squirrels were capering.

To be easily platitudinous, spring is about the most reassuring thing in the world. It's nice to know the engines of the cosmos are operating as they're supposed to, right on schedule, as predicted, and not taking time off to spend another week in Hawaii.

I can express a twinge of regret for those Canadians who have chosen to live in the rain shadow of the Olympic Peninsula. Spring must mean so much less to those people. Just a smear in actuality, a casual drift out of cloudy days and into days of less cloud. Lacking drama. Spring for the rest of us is gutsy. (No, that was not a typo, although, for perverse reasons, I recall one of my favourite typos. In the tattering remnants of Hurricane Hazel, back in the first season when hurricanes were given names, the *Calgary Herald* reported that the hurricane was blown out, but there were guts all around southern Ontario.) Anyone can love July; it takes more nerve to face a setback in spring's onset in April when the wind seems capable of flensing the hide from our cheeks.

Paragraph by paragraph as I write spring is deteriorating. It darkens the theme. I had meant to say something about the sublimity of exactitude, how clear the markers show up, and already the day looks as savage as November.

Ah, but spring's changeful aspect, then, its promise, and then its promise withheld, can equally be the subject. It can be difficult to believe even now the pasque flowers are calling upon their reserves of energy to thrust themselves up through the blanket of snow. Masked mountains look like old photographs and recall, as old snaps do, the forgotten rituals of spring. In the days before panchromatic film the mountains around Banff tended frequently to look like mist-shrouded braes in Scotland or the fog-enhanced paintings of the Hudson River school. Today, as small flake snow hovers everywhere, the landscape looks as grim as Edward Landseer's portrait of the dog who has followed the wounded stag into the highland moors, "and will nae leave his stalk until his master comes."

Here came the promise of green, and now it is greying down again. Wilful, scarcely capricious, a hammer jolt to our sense of reality.

The tempos of spring are initially subtle. We note the lengthening measure of the days. The day before yesterday it was still light enough to read at 7:30 in the evening. Today's difference is not greatly marked, but still remarkable. The amount of tickling under snow today seems insufficient to force the rebirth of the world, and it will seem almost as meagre tomorrow. There is an ancient recording of *Bolero* conducted by Ravel, and its forceful slow insinuation in its first four or five minutes seem equivalent here. Conductors other than the composer seem to increase the tempo far more rapidly. *10* would have been a different movie with Ravel's own performance. But that's how spring can come to us. Stately measures of an ominousness, bar-by-bar and phrase-by-phrase altering to suggestions of animated richness, until at last an ecstasy of crescendo is upon us.

In the Rockies we shall not know it is here in its full force until suddenly we are surrounded by burned faces, the result of skiers basking on the upper slopes of Whitehorn or Lookout, having decided the days are too wonderful for full exertion. Spring probably sneaked up on them as well, for they forgot the Paba-10, and wouldn't have packed it in their bum bags anyway.

An easy winter, such as the one we have just come through, makes spring fulfill its drama just as surely as harsh winters. We love the upsurge of liquidity in the green world no less because we have not felt the brunt of blizzard.

There are still two months to go before the green capes of poplars and aspens are again worn in fullness. Which is why, again, I think of Ravel's own performance of *Bolero*. The insinuations of spring are upon us now, but it can take so long for its eager presence to make itself known completely. Not only that, but it shall be three months before we can walk very far above Banff. People from the coast sometimes say they feel sorry for the rest of Canada for spring does not arrive so truly elsewhere in the country. But once the Fraser Delta people have had their spring – in a week or two – they have only a sustaining summer to look forward to. They miss the mania which can surround the surprise of a bud here, a bloom there, an unfurling of a leaf.

"Springtime in the Rockies"? O, it should have been a longer song, if it were to contain all the joy and all the theatre we know the season can contain.

23 MARCH 1983

One of the manifold pleasures of reading the Sunday *New York Times* was to peruse each week the editorial which coincidentally occupied, on a slightly larger scale, the same space as this.

A pleasantly voiced speaker, a cross between Robert Frost and H. Gordon Green, would ignore the hurly-burly of auto workers' strikes, the threats of cruise missiles, rising costs, and talk instead of the joys of seeing moles under his lawn again, or how the mellowness of afternoon was returning to his world, or pursue the gentility of idle walking.

I never determined whether the comments were written by one staff writer, or whether the task was rotated amongst all the staff of the editorial department. It seems to me there was so much consistency in voice it must have been one person. Now I rarely see the Sunday *Times*, and I'm not certain if the page continues yet to explore what are, in a sublime balance of things, the more important themes, the constant reassurance of the world that it is rotating and revolving in its old cycles just like it's supposed to be.

A glance at the reality of this May obliged me to note that the leaves are just four or five days ahead of schedule, a significant difference in the life of a plant, for it means that its growing season is extended by something like three per cent. It may not seem a lot to a species which might sustain itself for four or five hundred years, but if it were repeated year after year, just that slightly greater growing season, our ecology here could be quite different. Not so different as to allow apple trees, perhaps, but maybe maple trees.

Jimmy Simpson, the one we used to call Big Jim, was a careful noter of such phenomena. Perhaps his most idiosyncratic observation was that the Earth had wobbled itself out of its orbit, at least as the world was seen from 107 Bear Street. Those of us who live under the winter shadow of Sulphur Mountain try to keep track of the day when the sun disappears behind Sanson Peak, and again the day it first clears the top of the mountain in its arc. Jimmy, who lived beneath that shadow for close to seventy winters, some time about 1960 indicated that the sun's path had altered – or that the Earth's path had altered. That such a perturbation of the globe was not visible elsewhere – Stonehenge or Karnak, for example – seems not to have troubled him. Banff was merely, as some of us have long suspected, slightly out of joint with the rest of the world.

It was important for Jimmy to keep track of such things, as it is for all of us, to know with a fair degree of observational exactitude just when the deer are likely to moult, when catkins are supposed to appear on willows, when the cotton is likely to fill the air again.

The constant world of signs – by which I mean nature's emblems – keeps us in touch, and it would seem that in a world of information, data processing, and statistics we are in danger of being more out of touch than we were when there was less information.

On winter days, back when the skating rink was properly out-of-doors, the boy-scientists in us used to observe the phases of the moon on a daily basis. We knew from experience which way the moon moves against its celestial background. When the space age blossomed twenty-five years ago there was supposed to be a new awareness of the sky. I doubted that the awareness had sunk in very much. To test my proposition I asked some thirty friends and acquaintances if the moon, a) stayed in the same relative place all month, b) moved forward in the sky toward the sun, and then passed it, or c) if it moved backwards from the sun until it laggingly caught up to the sun.

In the new sophistication of the space age the people I asked gave answers that fell very close to chance. In other words most of them were guessing. One third of them thought the moon always stayed in about the same place in the sky, which is to say it had no phases. The other twenty people guessed that it moved either forward or backwards, and they were about evenly split in their opinion. They knew less of the night sky than a Greek or Wyoming shepherd. So much for sophistication.

But the leaves are coming back to the trees again. Four or five days early. It portends something, but not too much I venture. An easy winter past is what it more likely signifies than a long hot summer to come.

18 MAY 1983

It's a little difficult to determine what the reaction of the boys in the Halfway Hut is going to be when they hear of the recent death of Sir Norman Watson.

You'll remember the ghosts who play poker there regularly; they're the subject of a fine piece of verse by John Porter which appears in *Timberline Tales*. It would seem a certainty ere long Sir Norman's ghost will also come a calling in the Ptarmigan Valley. Sir Norman was probably not a poker player; that fact is unlikely to inhibit his ghost's actions.

Facts rarely got in the way of Sir Norman.

I apparently met Sir Norman when I was a tyke. I've been hearing stories about him for years, so many years I wasn't certain I wished to meet the man when the opportunity arose. I thought it might be preferable to live with the imaginary vistas I had dreamt him into. Sir Norman, however, was everything in life tale-tellers said he was; imagination could not improve upon him.

It was an afternoon in the Post Hotel. Sir Norman had invited Cliff and Catharine up for lunch, and Catharine said to me, "You've never met Sir Norman! Well, you must see him for yourself. You must come along."

Sir Norman, who by then was approaching eighty I reckon, was fulminating in the fashion he was famous for. Life in London, since the Indians and the Pakistanis had taken over, was scarcely worth the living, he suggested. It was a pity the Empire wasn't what it used to be, when an Englishman knew where he stood, and everyone knew where an Englishman stood.

He lectured us. Or, at the least, he spoke unremittingly for more than an hour and half. He pointed out the new wallboard in the lounge room of the hotel, and said forthrightly he thought it an improvement over the logs it concealed. Catharine was aghast. "But you'd know that about log buildings, wouldn't you, Cliff," he said. "The problem with them is simply this: after you've built the building, you have to build another bulding in them to make them habitable."

He did not disappoint us, or he did not disappoint me. In due course he got on to his favourtie topic, "The Alpine Cow." "People laugh when I mention 'the alpine cow,'" he grumbled, "but they have never understood what stimulated my interest in it." (Sir Norman's idea, hatched in the 1930s, was for imported Swiss and Austrian cowherds and farmers, who would dwell in picturesque alpine style buildings, to inhabit the Ptarmigan Valley. They would keep cows in their lower floors, like the Swiss, and in the summer the cows would graze the highlands of Boulder and Deception Passes.)

"I believe the alpine cow will lead to a marked improvement in the quality of food served in lodgings of the Canadian Rockies. With good dairy products available – good milk, good butter, good cheese – there will inevitably be an improvement in the quality of other food served. It would be so simple, and so effective," he concluded.

Later, when we were returning to Banff, we mentioned how happy we were to have had yet another lecture on the subject. "I never dared ask him how the cows intended to get along with the grizzlies," Catharine said. "But facts never meant much to Sir Norman."

More recently Cliff has suggested it would be appropriate to reintroduce the Sir Norman Watson Trophy Race now, an annual event once held in the highlands of the Slate Range, a race that takes its entrants from Skoki Lodge over Deception Pass and across Ptarmigan Lake, coming to a finish line near Temple Lodge. In today's keen langlaufing world many capable racers are around who could combine the climbing and downhill aspects of the race superbly.

Sir Norman also spoke that day of his dream of a network of lodges and backcountry cabins that would have developed Skoki, the Red Deer Valley and the Pipestone too. In the summer of 1939 packhorses carried nails, lumber and glass for windows up to the Natural Bridge for one such cabin, but the outbreak of the war in September curtailed the construction.

The afternoon we spoke to him he was still making new plans, and one sensed he would like to see it. Tweedsmuir was no longer Governor-General of Canada. It must have been a sorry day for Sir Norman when Vincent Massey became Governor-General, for it meant an Englishman no longer had a sympathetic ear in Ottawa.

8 JUNE 1983

Newshawks, to use a term now slightly antiquated, used to alarm Banff Avenue every afternoon with their calls of CAL-ga-Ree HA-ruld. It's a vanished element of the aural environment, not only in Banff, but universally.

The din of cars and the vanishing pedestrian have diminished to the point of no return the street calls George Gershwin made such good use of in *Porgy and Bess*.

The kids who sold *The Albertan* were more cautious in their cries than *The Herald* newsboys, if only because they were on the street in front of the Mount Royal Hotel as early as 6:45 am and no one, no matter how keen he may be on the arts of folk expression, would wish to hear raucous little kids calling and crying their wares to the world.

I became a newsboy when I was about six. For the cost of one of today's *Heralds* I went into business. Fifty cents bought twenty papers which could be sold for a nickel each. It took about an hour and a half to sell twenty papers.

The competition was severe: four or five kids on the west side of Banff Avenue in the 100 block, three or four kids on the east side (then, as now, considered the inferior side of the street, even by an eight year old entrepreneur). The turf was zealously defended. From Ted Evans' Meatateria to the Harmony Drugstore, from J.D. Anderson's to the Hub Cafe, no other newshawk was allowed to enter another's turf unless he had papers left after his "competition" had sold out. Then, only then, would momentary enmity be forgotten, and friendship reestablish itself.

Twenty papers yielded a dollar in sales, of which fifty cents would be kept for the financing of the morrow's sales. (Parents would bankroll only the first day's venture. Were you so casual as to spend not only your profit but your capital too, then you'd have to arrange your financing through other channels.) Fifty cents could obtain admission to the Lux, buy a bag of Scotch mints, and leave enough change for two comic books (or one Classic comic book and a Malted Milk chocolate bar).

The papers arrived by Greyhound. The route kids got theirs first; then we got ours, cash on the line from Lorne Orr, no credit for anyone except the route kids who were expected to pay up once a week. Then it was a dash to the street to get there first. The kid who arrived at the distribution centre (behind the Mount Royal) first would get his papers first, and be on the street a full fifteen minutes before the last kid. Hence there was a fair amount of competition to arrive early. Hence there was a fair amount of time to fool around, for some kids would arrive as much as an hour and a half before the bus was expected, and then the bus could be up to half an hour or forty-five minutes late.

Two or three summers' faithful salesmanship could work a guy up to a good corner, like the King Eddy or the Quaker, where you could not only sell papers faster, but you could also sell more of them.

Capitalism's ghastly spectre manifested itself to us my second summer. The wholesale cost of *Heralds* went up to three cents each, but we still sold them for a nickel. We had to invest sixty cents to realize a dollar, and we could no longer double our money. We thought it very unfair. If we recast the situation into today's infatuation with percentages, the wholesale cost of the merchandise had risen by twenty percent, and our profit had decreased by ten. There was talk of a strike. A newsboy's revolt. It never happened.

6 JULY 1983

Samuel E.S. Allen of Philadelphia on August 11th, 1894, undertook what I now consider the single greatest day of Canadian Rockies exploration. Most people who recall Allen at all link him, properly, with Walter D. Wilcox, but Wilcox publicized himself so well we tend to think Allen was tail to the Wilcox horse rather than the other way around.

Allen wrote three articles which appeared in *The Alpine Journal;* Wilcox wrote a book which contained his magnificent photographs. Readers seek out the Wilcox book frequently, the Allen material but rarely. Wilcox visited the Rockies frequently after the summer of 1894. Allen developed dementia praecox in the late 1890s and was institutionalized for nearly five decades before his death in 1944.

Wilcox, I believe, envying Allen's skills and determination, belittled his companion's accomplishments. It is a story we shall never know in detail, for its actors are now dead some thiry-five years, and documents are scarce.

To return to Samuel Allen's greatest day: he could not persuade his companions to join him when he set out for a day's ramble. The lads – they were all in their young twenties – had made their camp in Paradise Valley close to the base of Sentinel Pass. Allen walked up the trailless Paradise Valley to the base of Wastach Pass, crossed the pass to Eiffel Lake, then made his way to the summit of Wenkchemna Pass, descended to the Eagles' Eyries, then ascended by the rubble covered glacier he discovered there to the summit of Opabin Pass, descended by the glacier on the pass's other side to the region we now call Opabin above Lake O'Hara.

Engaged in just such a history lesson last week as we were approaching Wenkchemna Pass from Moraine Lake, we decided to undertake the Allen Route in part and proceed to Lake O'Hara.

After Allen had reached the O'Hara basin he sauntered the meadows briefly, then made his way back by the three passes he had crossed in the morning to reach camp in Paradise Valley before dusk. If Allen could cross six passes in one day, it seemed to us we could cross two passes with time to spare.

Our day's experience led me to enhance greatly my view of Allen's stamina. We were on trails for half our distance. We knew where we were going. I had covered half the distance before. I knew the geography reasonably well. Allen didn't know his destination. Only vaguely could he know where he was going. The forays of Allen and his companions in the Lake Louise, Paradise and Wenkchemna regions had informed his knowledge of the Alberta side of the Great Divide.

We lacked proper equipment for our excursion on the glaciers, but we were never in dire risk. The crevasses were all visible, and we could proceed with caution. Our caution impeded our pace, and our effort to skirt the bergschrund by going up a spur of Mount Hungabee was thwarted by slurries of gravel slithering down the slope we were trying to go up. Finally from above we saw a substantial bridge across the schrund, a route that could have saved us an hour or more of fiddling around.

It was seven o'clock before we reached Lake O'Hara, and it was only through the generosity of mountain friends we managed to get back to the car at Moraine Lake by nine o'clock.

Had we gone on to finish in a day what Samuel Allen had accomplished I think we might have reached the base of Sentinel Pass by dawn. That is if we were still able to walk, and find our route in the darkness. But we would have been on trails most of the way.

The veil of time and the mist of madness conceal Samuel Allen from us, but in his long day he brought to us the upper region of the Wenkchemna Valley, Wenkchemna Pass, the Eagles' Eyries, Opabin Pass, and the Kootenay Route to Yoho Park. No greater day of accomplishment? I'm certain of it now.

7 SEPTEMBER 1983

"He's a real main streeter, isn't he?" the woman with me said, as we were walking back down the hill from a visit with Charlie Reid.

"A main streeter?" I asked.

"You know: a man who has his shop on main street, and just loves to be part of the passing parade. Small town main street. Knows everybody in town. Everybody in town knows him. Welcoming hand out. Dapper as can be. A main streeter."

She was a film maker who had never met Charlie before, and it was after Charlie had sold the drugstore. I thought it a comment that summed Charlie most succinctly.

Charlie was quietly proud of his long position on Banff Avenue. He told me one time he probably held the record for the longest stay on Banff Avenue. I thought it over and guessed he was probably correct. I mentioned it to someone else who said, "I guess he forgets he used to work for Mrs. Gourlay, and she still attends to the cash register." But Charlie probably put in many more hours on Banff Avenue than Mrs. Gourlay has. (I don't intend to make an issue of this. That's not the point.)

Two favourite stories about Charlie:

The first concerns his habit of not making a bank deposit every day. One evening he did make a deposit. It was probably a week or ten days of revenue. When he had it all together – maybe a thousand dollars, maybe more; I'm not even sure when this happened – he put it in a brown paper bag to take with him. Outside the door he noticed his newspaper racks were still on the sidewalk, so he put the bag down while he moved the racks back into the shop. The task accomplished, he locked the door and went home.

The following morning, about to open the shop, he saw the brown paper bag sitting on the sidewalk. Mildly cursing such people as would litter the street with garbage, he was about to toss it in the waste disposal box when it occurred to him the bag had a slightly familiar look.

The other story is about Charlie and his close friend Carl Rungius, Banff's great wildlife painter.

In the 1940s a number of the town's gardeners had learned vitamin pills could nourish the plants in their rock gardens. They were obtaining their pills from Charlie.

Carl had gone to a doctor because he was feeling a little run down, and the doctor said he needed some vitamin pills, so he took himself to see Charlie.

"How do I take them?" Carl asked.

Charlie knew Carl was an avid rock gardener, so he assumed Carl wanted the pills for his plants. "Oh," said Charlie, "it's quite simple. Just dissolve one in a gallon of water."

"My gott," said Carl in his guttural German accent, "how do people ever manage that?"

Charlie told me it was a wonderful moment. Carl's eyes were agog at the predicament of drinking four or five gallons of water a day, and it was a bewildering moment for him before Charlie realized it was Carl who needed the vitamins and not Carl's forget-me-nots.

Charlie Reid: a real main streeter.

15 FEBRUARY 1984

A woman asked me this past week what she should take into Skoki. After a balaclava, I thought, stories are the most important things. Lacking enough stories to last for two evenings, you'll find yourself talking about television programmes, and you'll start to wonder why you spent three or four hours getting to a place that lacks television.

Every time we go to Skoki we carry along the same old stories, but each trip to Skoki seems to provide a new story which becomes part of the accumulation. The greatest thing about stories is their lightness and portability. I've seen people with seven kilo packs, but they've packed a couple of gross of stories into the map flap, and the pack seems inexhaustible.

There was that time, for instance, when Ike Mills took the stove into Skoki with his dog team.

Ike Mills was a world champion dog racer. Used to race for the Strongheart Trophy out on Minnewanka. Ike's local dogs used to beat the import dog teams, and the movie company that was here making the Strongheart movies put up the trophy, and Ike used to win it.

Ike had a great sense of drama. When he and his dogs were taking the new airtight into Skoki he got to thinking about how he ought to arrive, so a couple of miles from the lodge he stopped the sled. In fifteen or twenty minutes he'd rigged up the new stove on the top of the sled, and within ten minutes after that he's gathered kindling, and managed to find enough green timber around so he could have a blazing fire going in the stove, smoke pouring profusely from the chimney.

With all his preparations made, Ike mushed his dogs once more, and, like a Mississippi riverboat making its way up to St. Louis, stove, Ike, dogs, sleigh, and smokestack arrived belching at the lodge.

Dreams of a great jest realized were apparitionally forming in his head as Ike and his team came across the last few knolls. Wouldn't the people at the lodge think things were just great, he was hoping, and everyone would love his spectacular arrival. The only thing he didn't count on was what happened. All those best laid plans and preparations: when he steamed into the lodge vicinity, there wasn't anyone to greet him. Everyone had gone off to Merlin Lake for the day, and he had to sit in his loneliness, contemplating whether he should go back and do it all again when they returned.

The team had spilled the sled a couple of times earlier on the trip into the lodge, and the stove was banged a little out of shape by the spills it had suffered. The heat in the stove meant it took a little while for the stove to cool down, and afterwards the boys had to hammer the stove into a semblance of its former shape.

Maybe he would have done better to take a story along.

That's a story from the 30s, but new stories are also accumulating. A couple of years ago, when we were into Skoki, we were pleasantly thrilled by the sight of "The Sons of Sir Norman," a clutch of skiers from the Lake Louise area who had skied into the lodge the night before, carrying among other things lawn chairs, an umbrella, and a tape recorder so they could listen to Sir Norman's type of music. Said Cliff, the only thing he recalled Sir Norman ever listening to was *Begin the Beguine,* which he used to listen to hour after hour.

But the sight of those lads out on the snow sitting in their lawn chairs managed to evoke sufficient of the perversity of mountain zeal to keep us quite amused.

Quite admirable, I thought, to ski in darkness with an angular tubular aluminium contraption on the back, merely to evoke joy in other people.

But it may be that Ike and the Sons of Sir Norman got enough kicks out of their capers for themselves alone, happy in their own sense of audience.

14 MARCH 1984

I have known about Sidehill Gougers so long I feel I never knew a time when I did not know about them.

Hence with some alarm I discovered I know almost nothing about them, nothing more than the few facts that all of us know: that in some cases their left legs are shorter than their right legs, and the members of that ilk of Gouger run in a counter-clockwise direction, that those whose right legs are shorter than their left run about slopes in a clockwise direction. (Or is it the other way around? I have the same difficulty with high and low pressure systems.)

But when someone asked me a day or two ago whether Sidehill Gougers are unique to the Canadian Rockies or whether they are also to be found in the American Rockies, whether they are to be found in mountainous areas of all North America, or if they can be found throughout the Western Hemisphere, I had to admit my ignorance. About the only thing that was certain – and its certainty is doubtful – is that Sidehill Gougers seem to exist only in the New World. The German with whom I was conversing and his wife had never heard of them. The suggestion is clear: Sidehill Gougers are principally of the New World.

But my knowledge of their natural history is quite incomplete. I don't know if their direction – cyclonic or anticyclonic – is gender based. Do the males go in one direction and the females the other? Do mother Gougers have problems with their litter, with half of the kids going in one direction and half headed off the other way? Has speciation and specialization occurred for different altitudes? Are there Gougers of the alpine and the subalpine? Have they adapted to variations in circumstance? Are there Gougers with variations in their leg length difference who have adapted to slopes of different pitch?

I've heard Gougers are violent, irascible, and tetchy. It's about the only other fact concerning them which seems to be known. The second thing I learned about them is that when you are chased by a Gouger you run in the opposite direction, for the Gouger will not be able to pursue you.

But how large are they? Are they goat-sized? Pika-sized? Marmot-sized? Are their coats long and shaggy? Do they have variations in pelage dependent upon their altitude? Do they ever reach impasses? It's possible to imagine easily a circumstance in which a slope suitable for a Gouger could lead inevitably to a cliff and the Gougers – given their predilection to one direction – would have no choice but to stop at the point where slope gives way to cliff, and have no means of turning back and spend the rest of their days in accelerating starvation.

To be clear about my concerns: has anyone ever studied the mythogenesis of the species? Do we know where Sidehill Gougers were first described? Is there any literature on the species' origin?

I've blithely assumed – since I've known about them all my life – that everyone knows about them. It had never occurred to me that it's only those few of us who live in mountainous realms who are familiar with them. Do they hibernate? It's a fairly serious question, since I've never heard of skiers encountering them anywhere in the Rockies during ski seasons. Or – more likely – do Gougers have more mobility in the winter through some sort of adaptation to snow?

If anyone should encounter anywhere on a trail anywhere in the mountain national parks a Gouger colony this summer, I hope he or she will get in touch with me. If anyone can come back with a photograph suitable for publication, I'm willing to put up the usual reward for such things.

I suspect – but don't know for sure – Gougers may be an endangered species. I heard many more instances of sightings about them thirty years ago. Are they being forgotten? Does anyone really care?

13 JUNE 1984

Calamity seems to have diminished in the past decade as a part of our mountain lives.

Floods of the Bow used to occur just as regularly as the 24th of May came around, and we could be certain the river would flood its banks and swirl about Bow Avenue for ten days or more in June. Sweepers would lose their rootedness in the bank in the strong current, and during the flood season a tangle of jammed trees and branches would knot themselves about the footings of the bridge. The river's mayhem reminded us of the wild world that surrounds us. Now the Bow rises slowly over a month or two, and then it subsides in three or four weeks, and its rage is contained every year within the river's banks.

It's been seven or eight years now since we've had days so smokey the sun's light had turned to a dull reddish-orange, and no calamitous conflagration has broken out among the forests near at hand since the Vermilion Pass fire of 1968. Small fires have broken out, but nothing has dramatized forest fire for sixteen years. It's an unusual aspect of forest life, the historians tell us, for most of the Bow Valley used to show evidence of recent fires, and the monoculture of lodgepole pine is something we've created since the arrival of the railway a century ago.

Mute evidence of the huge avalanches of the winter of 1969-70 still shows itself in the broadened paths of slide tracks on Mount Whymper and in the heaped-up debris of the runouts near Ross Lake, but we haven't had a big enough slide to close the highways for a week or more since then.

It's quiet calamity now. It's a gradual, slow drying up and withering. Rarely visible, rarely spectacular.

These things are related. The lack of floods in the past decade is a result of the increasing density of the forest and forest floor in the Bow River drainage. We may have had less snow, but the snow that's fallen has melted more slowly and the moss and duff have held it captive for longer periods. No longer can spring's hot days arrive and the snow all melt in ten days or so, whoosh! Fewer fires have resulted in fewer floods.

Smaller snow accumulations in the winter and fewer storms result in fewer avalanches, and if the slide paths gradually choke up again with willows, once again the snow cannot melt off calamitously. Smaller snowfalls, fewer avalanches, less snowpack, rarer floods.

To the east, on the prairies, the lack of disaster in our mountain lives is turning into one big disaster for the farming communities. The same circumstance that brings storms to the mountains and creates avalanche conditions brings snow to the stubblefields and replenishes ground water. Two or three blizzards in a winter can go a long way toward staving off drought. All this long, hot July that tanners and hikers have found so wonderful is obtained at an awful price.

We could do with more calamities. The floods we think of as disasters can also be replenishing. The forest fires we consider rampant and ravaging destruction are the creators of open range, more rapid runoff, and destroyers of disease. The avalanche wantonly sweeping the mountain slope betokens larger snowfalls, more moisture-laden snow.

Mountains exaggerate most natural elements that they host. Plant and animal life scatter themselves in greater diversity as adaptation demands particularly of circumstance. Storms concentrate in valleys or on the high and exposed peaks and plateaus. A decade of the sort we seem to be in the middle of rarely occurs, but its accumulating destructive power is more wanton than the smaller localized calamities.

No one would wish to be a prophet of doom, but it's time nature started acting a little more cantankerously.

8 AUGUST 1984

With no intent to compete with the services at the Cenotaph on Sunday, I agreed to lead a walk through the Tunnel Mountain Cemetery on Remembrance Day. As a traditionalist, I knew the Cenotaph services would occur at the eleventh hour on the eleventh day of the eleventh month.

Diane McIvor and I had agreed Remembrance Day would be an appropriate day for a memory walk, and I thought one pm wouldn't conflict with the day's more serious ceremonies. I felt a note of chagrin within myself when I started out to meet whatever small group of people might join me for the cemetery walk just at the moment the Calgary City Police Pipe Band came skirling down Banff Avenue and the veterans marched past on their way to the memorial beside the bridge. I meant no disrespect, and, should I lead a group through the graveyard some future Remembrance Day, I'll set it later in the afternoon.

Close to the time of the Armistice of the First War, near eleven am on Remembrance Day last Sunday, I happened to be looking at a poignant reminder of the young men who died in France almost seventy years ago. In the collections of the Alpine Club of Canada is a small object framed in oak, an ACC Red Book – the list of members of the Club – which had been found in a German trench after the siege at Vimy Ridge. Some young, unknown climber had carried with him that precious object, a memory of mountains and mountain friendships. He likely died in one of the waves of battle in that terrible struggle. Now, sixty-six years after that war ended, I found it a small but moving testimony to that spirit of sacrifice that burned in soldiers' hearts.

The cemetery in snow was quietly beautiful, solemn, gracious, and warm. I jested that since the Bow Valley Naturalists has been around for seventeen years now, it's trying to create programmes appropriate to its aging membership. Long hikes of 400 metres or so, with an elevation gain of perhaps ten metres. But I love that cemetery so much, I relished the opportunity to share my enthusiasm for it. It's probably the nicest cemetery in Canada, I think.

Finding some of the graves I wanted to find was made a touch more difficult because of the snow, but we found most of the ones I'd considered: Mr. and Mrs. Greenham, Bill Davie, A.O. Wheeler, Sandy Thompson, George Brewster, John Murray Gibbon, but the snow inhibited my search for William and Mary Warren. Sometime, I hope, Bruce Beattie and I can go up to the cemetery together, and I'll strap the trusty Uher to my arm so I can record his comments. There's a whole cluster of Beatties over by the Lerne's Hill side of the cemetery, and I'd like Bruce to tell me a little more.

One advantage of doing the ramble with a bunch of Banff folk, is that it's possible for the anecdotage to flow both ways, and I get to learn just about as much as I disburse.

Because I'd chosen to do the walk on Remembrance Day, I got to thinking maybe we should have a day on the calendar when we can acknowledge not only the members of the armed forces who gave up their lives to wars, but all our ancestors, forerunners, and precursors.

The intimacy and scope of the Tunnel Mountain Cemetery makes a walk among the ancestors a little easier. I imagine trying to locate the formers of Calgary consciousness in Calgary's graveyards could be difficult: it's not as though they're all so close together that a slow walk can take you past most of them.

Wiping the snow from the headstones and the plaques made our small ceremonies in the graveyard acts of a different sort of reverence. I've never walked through the graveyard when the plaques were all frosted and dimmed. Here and there we could see where other pilgrims had trudged through the snow in their quest to find a meaningful memory. It gave the day a different tone for me, and one I cherished.

14 NOVEMBER 1984

As surely as March is the leaf of February torn from the calendar, more seasonal changes seem to occur more quickly now than in any other period of the year except those magical three days between the 23rd and 26th of September when larch gold starts to kiss the alpine margins.

March started most rhythmically this morning when I heard a pileated woodpecker execute a paradiddle on a power pole as I strolled by. (No, I didn't recognize the particular sound of the pileated woodpecker; I saw the bird himself from a distance of about a metre. The most easily distinguished of our woodpeckers, he provided no chance for error.)

Then I heard several long drawn-out tones of male chickadees among the hovering spruce, and noted that the music of the month departs into new cadenzas. I think I heard some robins next, that fluted rush of notes is usually distinct, but a flurry of other activity interrupted my observations, so I can't claim I saw the first robin of spring.

The *Crag and Canyon* used to observe such things. Bill MacKenzie and I got our names in the *Crag* once about 1950 for our having observed the first robin. I think it may have been the first time I broke into print. The Spillers gratefully accepted our information, and we were keen to be the first the following year, but some other keen-eyed little kid managed to get a report in before we did.

In grade five we were splendidly located to observe other portents of spring. Our classroom that year was in one of the lower floor rooms of the high school auditorium with a southern exposure to the fire hall. The sun beat in on the white plaster and reflected its heat into a small thermal region, the snow vanished in the first week of March, and dandelions had burst up and bloomed by the occasion of the equinox.

The greatest event of spring was the formation of a lake in the depressed area around the flagpole which stood before the high school. Melting snow and other runoff created a pond with an area of a hectare or more. Night frosts would form ice a couple of millimetres thick, and a kid could walk tenderly on the undulating surface during the morning recess. By noon the sun would have thinned it so much it would be back to puddle again.

Acts of torment typical of high school kids included bearing girls or little kids out to the island at the base of the flagpole and then abandoning them there in a comic kind of Maypole ritual. The puddle was deep enough – up to forty centimetres – that not all rubber boots were high enough, and the matted grass and mud of the pond bottom was slithery and slick and just dangerous enough to walk on. A route to the northeast was the longest but safest method to get back to shore, but there was a great deal of delight in the importance of having been selected to be tormented. To have an annual feature of such attractive danger, risk and magic was an instance of incredibly good design.

I no longer seek out puddles in spring, but it seems to me we have fewer of the large and tantalizing sort now than when I was a kid, a consequence of the homogenization of the town. Larger storm sewers, paved streets and snow removal mean there just isn't as much snow around to melt into those great tubs. There has also been a gradual smoothing out of things. What meltwater there is no longer has as many depressions to gather in.

Seven to twelve year olds, those for whom dirty water is more attractive than clean, must still be able to find it when they wish, and it may be that puddles are inevitably larger and more attractive to little kids than they are to adults. I think I shall keep my eyes open this spring, if only to see if the playgrounds of the season are truly about us.

6 march 1985

I had the pleasure on the holiday Monday of being part of what has become a mainstay of holiday weekends – Trans-Canada gridlock. Not a furiously long caterpillar, it stretched only from that behemoth of a boulder at the Castle Mountain Viewpoint (the Mount Eisenhower Viewpoint?) to the Five-Mile Bridge (the 7.9 Kilometre Bridge? The one just beyond what used to be the the Five Mile Sand Pit. If you don't know, ask Bruce Beattie.)

The creep was slow but relatively constant, averaging between ten and fifteen kilometres per hour, but it allowed time for gracious observation of a field full of a murder of crows, pied by a tiding of magpies (and a digression on the venereal game that played on my mind briefly), the buttresses of luxurious green that seem to support the plated armour of Mount Ishbel, Ishbel herself agleam in the radiant light, the sweep of avalanche that sinusoidally curves down from Bourgeau, the play of light on the magnificent west face of the Sundance Range, the great maw of Hole-in-the-Wall (remembering again those photographs of the Masons who all trooped up there decades ago), to note that smaller but even more mysterious cave on the west side of Mount Norquay, and to look at the rolling surge of massif that curls and crests into Mount Edith, to look back to Castle and see another storm brewing in the basin formed by Helena Ridge.

Only the holiday gridlock, it seems, can slow us down sufficiently to see the magnificence of the Bow Valley in its after-storm, light-ragging, cloud-tattered shattered completeness and glory. Will I ever walk from the Five Mile Sand Pit to the Red Earth Creek parking lot? Not very likely. As a cyclist I usually remove myself from the mayhem pathway and take the Old West Road instead.

How much do I see when I'm driving the Trans-Canada at the usual pace of ninety kilometres per hour, I wonder, when I know what I'm looking at and what to look for? By comparison with what I saw in the slow glory of the creeping traffic on Monday, I must admit I don't see very much. How much then do visitors see when they don't know what to look for?

I know visitors don't know what to look for. That came home to me when I accompanied a group of museum curators to Lake Louise and learned that not one of them – all of whom had seen the Victoria Glacier before – realized there were glaciers at the far end of the vista. Intellectually they knew they were looking at the Victoria Glacier, but they saw no relationship between the glacier and the shape of the valley. Alert people, too, those museum people. If they didn't know what they were looking at, or how to read a mountain landscape, then how can we hope that the unaccompanied automobile visitor can make sense of what he's seeing?

Only by slowing visitors down, by providing bigger and better traffic jams on the highway, by cutting the shoulders off the Trans-Canada, by reducing the speed limit to twenty-five kilometres per hour and by ploughing up the macadam and resurfacing the road with gravel, among other solutions, will we be able to assure people will begin to see the mountains with something like the due respect that only slow time can underline.

I'm sure car tourists won't understand that what they see is a function of how slowly they travel, or that the faster they go and the greater distance they cover results in their seeing less. For those who wish to travel fastest and see the least, we should establish an ultra-high speed loop that will take them north from Medicine Hat, east to Brooks, south to Foremost, and then back to Medicine Hat. But if they come here to see and, we hope, appreciate something, then they should be prepared to take it at the pace it deserves.

Perhaps only a local could thoroughly appreciate the richness of travelling so slowly down the Bow Valley while storms gather and disperse. But I wish the jam had been longer and moved more slowly yet. It was that rich.

7 AUGUST 1985

If anyone has forgotten how heavy the cone load on the conifers was last summer, much of the evidence is yet visible on the white spruce. Bowed heads and curved spines reveal that the treetops are bearing a lot more weight than the trunks are built for.

Conomancers – readers of meaningful signs in cones – were quick to alert me to such a proliferation of cones as a sure sign of the depth, harshness, and severity of the winter to follow.

I missed December and January, but I remember a little of November and quite a bit of February. November was severe, so hard I regretted the fact it turned pleasant the day I departed, so nice I wandered around Calgary in a thin sweater. About three days after my return from the antipodes it turned cold. But I am told that the solstitial months were as balmy as can ever be expected in these climes. It scarcely snowed in December and January, and the temperature many of those days was well above zero.

But up there on the tops of the trees the cones were massed for an onslaught of boreal furies, blizzards, storms, deep snow, chilblains, ague, and williwaws such as we have never seen.

Cones, apart from being useful to trees in the same way eggs are useful to chickens, form a large part of the diet of squirrels, nutcrackers, and grey jays. I admit to a liking for both squirrels and whiskey jacks, but I have never figured out why – in the minds of many people – nature should be particularly generous to those species. Enough cones still hang on the spruce to sustain a population of a million or more squirrels for a decade in this part of the Bow Valley. If nature singles out the arboreal species for bounty, while ignoring elk, deer, and moose, she is a bewildering and capricious spirit indeed.

A logical and meaningful reason for the trees to have overburdened themselves so extravagantly may yet emerge. In my own capricious way, I surmise the trees had some prescient awareness of what was going to occur to their kin across from the Catholic Church. "When you see a great hulking mass of cones on the tops of the spruce, it means some contractor is going to get carried away and chop down many more trees than necessary," might be one way of putting it.

Or, more darkly, a profusion of cone clusters is a sign to the people of the Bow Valley that growth has gone too far. Nature is preparing a mighty forest that will rise up, like Birnam Wood, to march over lawns and take root in the alleys and byways of the town. If you're going to read signs, interpret them as grimly as possible. No one ever paid a fortune teller to find out that everything's coming up roses and daffodils when the promise of a vengeful nature and disaster can curdle consciousness more surely than lemon juice and cream together make a mess in a teacup.

In the meanwhile the squirrels have decided to go into the pyramid building business. For most of September and October they worked double shifts – with cone-and-a-half for overtime – to begin to shear the cones from the upper branches, but the squirrels got so weary with the work they gave up. It takes a lot of work to weary a squirrel. It was dangerous to go wood-walking last autumn because of the almost constant rain of cones from above. Cone piles the height of suburban garages have accumulated throughout the woods, and the squirrels are assured food throughout an ensuing glacial age.

That is, of course, the explanation. Cone loads are not merely short-term or medium-range forecasts meant for people to plan whether to hang around the northern forest for the winter. They are the first sign of the planet's intent to recover its northern continents with a couple of kilometres of ice, to erase the industrial cities of the Great Lakes, and to cleanse the landscape. Any explanation will do, won't it?

26 MARCH 1986

It's a slim connection, the centennial I'm celebrating this month. All I have to go on is that in June of 1936 the CPR sent a Fiftieth Anniversary Train a-chugging and a-puffing its way across the Shield country of Ontario, the plains of Manitoba, Saskatchewan, and Alberta, and into the mountains which are obviously their own state of mind.

Dave White, my grandfather, went down to the station with my aunt and uncle to see the train, and he said then that it was all very interesting, but that he didn't know just which train it was the fiftieth anniversary of. He said he'd thought he'd been on the first through train from the east, and it had arrived in April.

Two of his brothers had departed New Brunswick some ten to fifteen years before. They had made their way around Cape Horn on a sailing ship and arrived in British Columbia and gone looking for gold in the Cariboo country, so it wasn't all that unusual for the young man to head west to find out if the country had more to offer than New Brunswick did at the time, and seek his fortune as his brothers had.

Dave White got off the train in Banff then about a hundred years ago this month. There were already some McCardells and Woodworths and Keefes around here, among others whose names I can't quickly recall at the moment, so it wasn't as if he were anything like the first.

Dave had a cousin or uncle who was the Division Superintendent for the CPR, a man named Kavanaugh who worked in Canmore. Kavanaugh was a mighty man, so I've read, capable of lifting a rail onto a flatcar by himself. Rail in those days wasn't as heavy as it is now, but the feat would still be a bona fide test of strength. It wasn't at all strange that Dave got a job working for the CPR himself, section man at Cascade, out there by Muleshoe Lake, later to be renamed Sawback Siding.

After six or seven years of making his way by jigger between Cascade and Banff, Dave decided to move into town and start a store, the National Park Store, incorporated in 1894. His sisters Elizabeth and Margaret (Lizzy and Maggie, as nicknames of the period would have them) ran the store for him the first winter while he went to business school in Belleville, Ontario, so it wasn't until 1895 that he took the reins. By then others of his siblings had also made their way west, Dan and May among them. Finally only brother Jim was left in New Brunswick.

Somewhere along the line Dave became interested in the charms of Lade Bagley and he went so far as to give her a copper ring as a token of his affection. She went on to become Mrs. James Brewster, but she kept the ring, and some fifty years later Fern Brewster gave it to my aunt and uncle, who had never known that Dave White had expressed his interest in Lade.

As I say, I'm not sure exactly sure precisely when we're supposed to be celebrating this centennial of the Whites (or Whytes, it's a family which never quite learned how to spell its last name) in Banff. It may be today; it may already have flown right by; it may not be for another week or two. I'm not sure Dave would ever have considered the possibility that anyone a hundred years hence would give the least concern to his arrival.

I'm not even sure I know why he got off here. It may have been the Kavanaugh connection. It may be that he could afford a ticket only so far. There wasn't a lot here then to keep a person here. There wasn't a Banff Springs Hotel, and the government hadn't yet begun to build the bathhouses at the Cave and Basin.

But I'm glad he stopped off here. Maybe he looked around and said, "Hey, there isn't likely to be a more beautiful place anywhere. I'm going to stick it out in the Rockies." Anyway, I went down to the station a week ago, and looked around for a ghost and it felt good.

16 APRIL 1986

Where does bad weather come from?

It always comes from across the border. In Alberta our bad weather comes out of the Northwest Territories or Saskatchewan. We certainly don't manufacture it for ourselves.

Americans believe that Canada's principal export to the United States, away ahead of pulp and paper products and shakes and shingles, is shivers and blizzards.

In the Yukon I'm sure they think that most of the bad weather comes out of Alaska or maybe British Columbia.

I like to avert the American belief by telling them that all our worst weather comes out of Montana and Wyoming. We all sort of reach for our longjohns, I say, when we hear that a big one is brewing in the American Rockies. It stops them short. "But we say that all our worst weather comes out of Medicine Hat," they tell me, and I just let 'em know that that's bad American weather being turned away at the border.

Calgarians like to believe whenever there is bad weather in Calgary it must be absolutely awful up in the mountains. Back in the May storms when Calgary got closed down by the blizzard, I must have heard from dozens of Calgarians that life must have been completely pleistocene in Banff. They thought I was bonkers when I said that we got a little rain, but no snow to speak of. All of our worst weather, I said, usually comes out of Calgary, but Calgary gets it first and worst. They think I'm just a curmudgeon and a Calgaryphobe about such things.

It was much easier in the days when mythic forces could be attributed to the gods. To imagine the North Wind as a bona fide malevolence with a keen wit and a harsh tone, the picturing of huffin' puffin' hard blowin' cheeks extended gustiness, meant you didn't have to locate him on any side of any particular border.

He could just be a force.

Now that we have provincial boundaries and international borders, and even local subdivisions, means that in Canmore the downtowners can blame the storms on Cougar Creek and in Banff we can foist the responsibility on Valley View, and the North Wind doesn't have to take any of the charge.

We don't have enough local names for the winds who are our constant companions. We name Chinook, and that's it.

I don't know if we have williwaws, but we ought to. Williwaws are the sorts of confusing winds that occur in the mountains of the Yukon when the wind seems to come from all directions at once. New Zealand is nearly all williwaws.

My favourite wind name is out of "Pogo," the "Dread Blue Norther." He comes calling only once or twice a year, but you have to watch out for him when he decides to come a calling.

I always thought Mistral was a wonderful name for the wind, but a friend told me she had spent some time in Spain and that after a day or two she got sick and tired of the Mistral. The wind, however, didn't get tired of blowing, and kept it up for another month or so. You have to watch out for those evocative bits of poetry.

Perhaps it's a better name for a car than anything else.

What sorts of names can we suggest for our local winds? There's that funny wind that comes out of the southeast, a rare point on our particular wind-rose, and it normally bears some strange kind of rain with it. Since southeast is from a Banffocentric point-of-view more or less the Spray River, the winds from that direction might as well be Disprays.

Winds from the Northwest are also not very common. But it's a fortunate direction to come from in our point of view, if only because "Brewster" already sounds like a name for the wind. Perhaps a spelling change might be in order. I'd be more likely to go looking for the sheepskin chaps if the name of the wind were the Brooster.

Watch out, Matey, there's a Brooster a brewin' and it's headed right this way.

The soft winds and the sweet winds and the gentle winds of summer aren't the ones that need the names. It's the hard winds and the winter winds and the rough winds of autumn that bring us the portents of seasonal change, they're the ones we need to regard as not completely alien to us and the ones that really need to be named.

23 JULY 1986

The grade eight and nine rooms in the old three-storey brick Banff High School provided a particular pleasure each year at this time. The grade seven class in the basement provided only a glimpse of sunlight above the frosted glass and the withering geraniums.

But the grade eight room up on the top floor and under the wide eaves of the building and the grade nine room on the main floor gave an uninterrupted prospect of the Gully on Mt. Norquay. From the equinox to Thanksgiving, the blaze of poplars that settles in that dale was more than enough to distract my attention from Miss Chapman's Social Studies or Mr. Fisk's Science classes.

It was during one of Mr. Fisk's classes that I learned precisely how difficult it can be to create a coverup.

With my eyes drawn to that flare of gold, all my remaining attention dedicated to how handsome Norquay looked in autumn light, the limestone against the deep blue sky, I was about as far away from the topic of the class as any student could ever get without physically removing himself from the room. Bright autumn is fleeting, and the day was as green and gold and blue and grey as a day could be.

Only vaguely, as one might hear a mosquito through a drowsy sleep, I heard Mr. Fisk's intonation rise slightly as though he were asking a question. A moment after he affixed my name to the question I woke up, only to stare into a new and deeper space as though I were seeking the answer to the question.

"Well?" he asked.

"I'm considering it," I said, grabbing for any straw that might retrieve the question from the echoing and abyssal chambers down which it was retreating more rapidly than I could dash after it.

"Yes," I finally said, with what I hoped was assurance.

"Yes, what?" he asked.

"Well, of course," I added. Titters and giggles rose from the classroom's nether regions.

"Is that all you have to say about it?"

Did I murmur an apology? Did I say the poplars on Norquay looked wonderfully inviting, or that deeper and bleaker autumn was coming on and the moments of idylls would be rarer, and that for the moment the great outdoors deserved my full attention and that I ought not be diverted by something as repeatable as a science class? I should have perhaps, but grade nine students are rarely allowed such moments of wit.

"You weren't paying attention," he must have said, and I demurred to his judgment ere he proceeded to ask someone else the same question, a question I recall that had something to do with basic mechanics, something like defining the three classes of levers and providing examples. Not the sort of question to which one could answer with a "yes" or a "certainly."

An autumn never goes by now that I don't reflect on that anecdote. I look up towards the Gully, and I admire once again the particular boldness of Norquay's serried ranks of peaks, and I recall how wonderful a vista that classroom had, probably better than any other classroom I ever sat in. Certainly far better than any classrooms I sat in in Medicine Hat or the University of Alberta.

I see Ted Fisk from time to time, never when I happen to be looking up at Norquay, and he has probably long since forgotten the incident. But I wonder now – as I should have wondered then – if looking out the window at the richness of this landscape we live in might not have been a better action then than giving my full attention to the class. He might even agree.

1 OCTOBER 1986

April, the word, is related to aperture, and both words have to do with opening up.

Spring consists of many openings up. As the snow goes, the land opens up. It opened up in the Rockies this year with a flourish, almost the swiftness we once knew when plays began with curtains rising or opening up on a proscenium stage.

On Thursday last week I watched a small stalk of delphinium. At eight in the morning just a small nubbin of tightly furled leaves suggested anything was about to happen. Four hours later – almost as rapidly as time-lapse photography – five centimetres of small furry purple-green stalks of larkspur held four fans of fingered leaves extended for every jot of energy the hot sun could provide. It was another opening of another show.

Last year, you may recall, many perennials took the same fast leap into spring – just about as early. Frost nipped the early leaves, cut the stalks back to the ground. The particular larkspur to which I set my clock never recovered. Maybe they knew what the summer would hold.

Until about 1970, April used to be the month when Banff's liberating storekeepers would shake the sleep out of their eyes, yawn a couple of times, stretch in the sun, and begin considering opening up. Not until the Banff Springs got around to opening up, usually just before the 24th of May weekend, did the shopgirls get to work with ladder, the scrub brush, and the elbow grease to remove the Bon Ami that had opaqued the windows from the 20th of September.

What happened? Did Bon Ami go out of business? I've looked for it from time to time, remembering the chick on the package, but I haven't seen it for at least a decade. Maybe when they stopped making Bon Ami, Banff merchants didn't know what to use instead, so they decided to stay open all winter.

Apparently though, there may still be a trove of the stuff in a groceteria in south-western Alberta. A two-gross case may lurk in a groceteria in the village of Waterton. A photographic project which engaged a friend of mine one year took him to Waterton. He arrived there in mid-May and had a difficult time finding anything open. He found one open motel for lodging, and a small cafe provided him supper.

The next morning he believed he had slept away months of his life (about a hundredth of a Van Winkle, if that be the unit of sleep). Either that, or he had been transported in his sleep to Brigadoon. All the shutters had been flung open, the Bon Ami washed from the windows, the hoarding taken down, the shops were all open, the streets were full of milling tourists, the service stations manned. He knew it could not all have happened in the ten or twelve hours that had passed since he walked the street of Waterton looking for the action and had found it nowhere.

Yet there it was. Life had opened up in Waterton in the fashion of the elves arriving in the shoemaker's shop, or of the trolls descending upon the house of Halvor.

The other opening up is of the flesh. Ptarmigan and elk and goat moult slowly, but given the heat of the sun, the flesh of humans flashes forth in mere moments. One has to watch the aperture, or overexposure is easy.

I went down to inspect the opening up of the river that first hot spring day. It had opened up quite wonderfully.

But, what was more interesting was that the people had opened up too. A wonderful sort of camaraderie and cheer united the celebrants of spring in the ceremonies going on down there. For humans to even consider keeping up with magpies – who opened up in April, too – may be difficult, but the humans were chattering well.

8 APRIL 1987

Two rock climbers were well up the cliff on Mount Rundle, high over the eighth hole of the Banff Springs Golf Course, perhaps 500 vertical metres over the tee.

They had carefully glassed Rundle's great anticlinal dome of Palliser's limestone from the valley floor before they began their ascent, but to the best of their knowledge no one had undertaken any rock route on its wall before. They were checking out the possibility of a good route on a big wall close to Banff. Palliser limestone is among the best of local climbing surfaces, and the combination of cracks and ledges seemed to offer a splendid possibility.

From all the evidence – or lack of it – it appeared to be a virgin route. They saw not one sign that anybody had ever scaled the wall before. They had to clean out bits of loose rock and rubble, but there were no signs of pitons or any boot scuffing anywhere on their route.

Things went well. By the seventh pitch above the scree slope at the mountain's base, they hadn't met any unduly severe problems. Another forty or fifty metres and they would reach the top of the wall. It was beginning to recede to something like a seventy-degree angle, and small ledges were beginning to appear.

Tim belayed Dwayne as he manoeuvred out and onto a couple of ledges, using his free hand to discard pebbles and small boulders sitting on the upper ledge.

Tim failed completely to understand what happened next. Dwayne began laughing uproariously. What could possibly have happened that could be so funny?

Dwayne held up for Tim's inspection a bewildering token of evidence that they were not first on the wall: a shining white golf ball he had uncovered when he had dislodged one of the stones.

They looked down to the golf links 500 vertical metres below them. "One mean slice," one of them may have said.

Had some other climbers carefully and discreetly carried a Spalding in their packs to that height, there to conceal it beneath a rock so that eventually, knowing the ways of other climbers, they would discover it and be concerned or amused by the hyperbole of it all? Had some incredibly powerful links-swinger smashed his niblick into the dimpled projectile with Superman force, lofting it high above the treetops, higher than he had ever hit a ball before, and abandoned it there, taking the penalty stroke?

As thermals wafted warm air up from the valley, the climbers' laughter receded to silence, mystery, and the vaulted space doming the Bow Valley, and a couple of ravens who had ridden the currents up from the valley below wheeled about in the great tumult of the sky.

"A mystery solved!" Tim exulted. "We are the first."

Ravens, like all their corvine kin, admire bright and glittering objects. Clasped in a raven's bill, or more likely borne in its talons, the golf ball had been carried up by wings and a thermal and concealed in a cleft between a rock and the wall.

The rest of the climb went easily, and by the end of another pitch they had finished it off, and descended to the Bow.

Climbers who make a first ascent on a new rock route get to name it. The names which identify the routes on the now famous Back of Louise climbing region have become a wonderful branch of poetry. After brief consultation and consideration, they decided their route had inevitably to bear the cognomen Hole-In-One.

15 JULY 1987

We're standing around in the Wapta parking lot (what shall we call Wapta now? Emerald Lake East? Sherbrooke Lake South? Lake McArthur North? Laggan West? Minnewakun Lake North-west?), waiting for the Lake O'Hara bus on Sunday morning. It's a little drizzly, the clouds hanging a bit like tapestry over Cathedral Mountain, but it isn't as if sheets of rain are falling, or that glebe is besmearing our glasses.

We're minding our own business, making sure we have the tea and the Gatorade, the rain-gear, and a change of dry socks, and we're looking at the muck that moves up from Wapta, when a fellow wanders up and says, "Do the experts on the Rocky Mountains know something we lesser mortals don't? Is there something happening up there that isn't visible from down here?"

I'm more or less a fair-weather hiker, but I rarely object to Canadian Rockies rain. Most of the time it's so light here that we don't have to face the lowered spears of umbrellas charging upon us like Bengal Lancers in the streets of Banff, so I tell the fellow O'Hara is a lot like the West Wapta region (Lake Louise, for those who don't know), it's so rich in micro-habitats, micro-landscapes, and micro-climates, that one doesn't have to rely upon the landscape macros for the excitement of the place. Then I reel into a spiel about how Tommy Link never saw the O'Hara region until the doctor's orders demanded he slow down, and he took only a hundred paces at a time, and then he saw the place for the first time.

It was not one of my more successful sermonettes. He wandered up to the bus shelter, and decided to question someone a little less rhapsodic, and two or three minutes later returned to his car with the kids and lit out for less delightful realms.

What did I know that he didn't? Not much. But the O'Hara region in light rain is delightful. After saying hi to the folks at the Lodge, we headed up to the Odaray Plateau, a place so delightful that a million golfers could only destroy it. (But then I side with those who believe a game of golf is the best way of ruining a good walk.) Meadow after meadow, the larch trees glistening with the silvery light that Carl Rungius believed was the most important feature of the Canadian Rockies, that unique and wonderful light that he as a painter learned he could never quite remember after he had spent four or five months in his Manhattan studio, and which summoned him back to the Canadian Rockies every year for forty-seven years.

Drama in the gentians we had been told we should look out for. Drama in the little brown bird that wandered dipper-like among the stream flowing out of Schaffer Lake, the bird we finally decided must be a water pipit. Drama in the raggle-taggle clouds shearing and regathering in front of Mount Huber.

When we ran out of time to do anything very adventurous later in the day, we turned adversity to advantage. I have heard about the Crystal Cave for a long time, but I'd never been there, so with little time left, I decided we should go there, though I didn't know where it is.

Ancient trails wandered and branched across the slope, yet in every case I chose the right one, and in fifteen minutes or less the gloomy portal of the cave loomed above us.

Three or four metres back from the cave entrance we observed the brick wall mortared into the quartzite. Fortunately my companion had read her Mary Stewart carefully and knew Merlin had been immured in the Crystal Cave, and she wouldn't have had it any other way.

That rock collectors dynamited the Crystal Cave – we don't know when – to collect quartz crystals may be the truth of the matter, but the brick wall is a fitting way to trap a wayward wizard, and part of the satisfaction of a fine and drizzly day.

29 JULY 1987

"I got an eagle on the Helen Lake course!" may be the type of exultant boast we will hear in the future if people come to accept my ideas of wilderness golf and orienteering golf.

I figure it's about a 120 par run from the Crowfoot Glacier parking lot up and into the Helen Lake cirque and back. It may be about a par 175 from Sunwapta Pass via Wilcox Pass to Tangle Creek. The wilderness golfer need only figure out where he wants to go, then drop his ball and blast off for the rough.

The hazards along the way to Helen Lake are quite wonderful. One mean slice on the way up the trail, your ball will bounce all the way down the slope to the Icefield Parkway, you'll add fifty or sixty strokes to the destination, but consider the pleasure you'll derive from golfing where people have never played before! Contrarily, a well executed hook at the point of the ridge where Mount Assiniboine is visible on a clear day will get you over the rocks ready to hit the 160 degree other direction. Of course your ball can bounce itself into the krummholzes above Helen Creek to disappear forever in shintangle.

Just along the trail, you will encounter both the dread marmots and the possibility of getting the eagle. But if you get the eagle you'll face a fine of $10,000 and a possible six month jail sentence. "Makes golf into a high risk sport, that's what it does."

Golfing in the alpine (one of those "biologied regions" we've been hearing about, Mr. Duck) may be subject to restrictions designed to protect the habitat. Teeing off from a sixty to hundred year old moss campion cushion will likely cause greater damage to the plant than can be repaired by replacing a divot. The upper sub-alpine or Hudsonian may be a practical limit. But lots of room in the sub-alpine will preserve the montane.

Wilderness golf will open up an entire new manufacturing realm for recreational outfitters. A backpack designed to provide pockets for three or four irons and three or four woods, while providing pockets for rain gear, lunch, and a compass and map, would be seen to be de rigueur. They'll love the challenge.

When wilderness golfers succeed in whittling scores down for the common destination areas of the Canadian Rocky Mountain peaks, I can foresee the keenest among them developing a new sport combining long distance orienteering with the Scottish game. Is it a par 875 from Banff to Lake Louise via Harvie Pass – Healy Pass – Gibbon Pass – Arnica Lake – Panorama Ridge? Will the backpack need straps for a tent, sleeping bag and white gas stove in addition to pockets for the niblick and the mashie? Will time become an element in the game too? A formula to assess score and time in combination? Since orienteering golf may require stream and river crossings far from bridges, the wilderness golfer will have to carry a good rope along in his pack too.

It may be days before a foursome starting from Laggan and headed for Fitzhugh ever see any of their companions. I mean is it better to head up the Ptarmigan for the more open territory or to stay to the deeply forested valleys of the Bow and the Mistaya, hoping to accommodate difficulty of lie by shortness of journey?

Other benefits will flow forth directly. Since national park trails forbid vehicles, golfers will be again obliged to walk, something many of them have not done since the advent of the golf cart. It will put exercise back into golf. Since both the golfing fraternity and sorority like to argue that "parks are meant for people," they'll be out there enjoying the parks in a way they have never considered it possible.

No longer will golfers have to consider the expense of hitting a hole in one. And Bankhead will be saved. Isn't it great what a little imagination can do?

19 AUGUST 1987

One shouldn't expect the Fenland Trail, bound on the north and east by the Trans-Canada Highway and the west access to Banff and on the south by the Canadian Pacific Railway, to be a quiet, serene place.

I was out there at dusk and later a few weeks ago, however, kind of hoping it would be fairly quiet. The Trans-Canada traffic, mostly trucks at that time of the night, was a dull and constant roar.

As we wheeled around back by Echo Creek in a counter-clockwise direction, the sounds of the town began to ascend. A freight train headed west rumbled by the grade crossing just as we reemerged on the highway, and for a couple of minutes we listened to axle squeak and coupler squawk as the train picked up speed and eventually disappeared into the night.

Further along Bow Avenue, we kept our ears open for sounds of beavers. A coyote appeared from the willows by the creek briefly and crossed over and into the trees back of the new hospital. The town's traffic sounds were becoming quite loud.

An unforeseen consequence of the act of mayhem of cutting down twice as many spruce trees in the hospital compound as was necessary is that the town sounds which the forest used to buffer and muffle can now freely waft right down Wolf Street unimpeded to contaminate the serenity of the river.

(That hospital is ugly, has far too large a parking lot, and its parking lot is over-lit is not my subject this week. I hoped we could have a hospital which might look as good as the bus depot.)

Banff now has a constant background roar, a combination mostly of traffic sounds, wheel whistle on pavement, bus rumble, and the unnecessary contribution of air conditioning units.

You're likeliest to notice it when you get down by the river and Bow Avenue. If you're downtown you expect noise, but it used to be only the launches going up the stream, and the passing trains that momentarily disturbed the peace of the river side.

I suspect what Banff needs is a carfew. Not a curfew, a carfew. There's an awful lot of driving around to no particular purpose in this town, and about the only thing the vehicles are putting out is too much noise.

I suspect people can get all their driving done between seven and nine in the morning and four and eight in the afternoon. After that you'd need a dispensation to be out on the streets of the town.

Consider the benefits. A nice quiet place to live and play and work. A virtual mall on Banff Avenue, something we've been waiting for since the time of the first Oberlander Report about twenty-five years ago. An exhaust-free atmosphere most of the day. A drop in the accident rate. A park-like feeling about the place.

With a carfew in place people would have to walk home from the bars, but they should probably be doing that anyway. (The unfortunate side effect of people walking home from bars is that they tend to shout meaningless things to each other, but better they should be speaking without meaning than driving without meaning.)

This town and this national park do not exist as part of the plan to burn up all the hydrocarbons buried under the prairies.

The sounds of the night, like the lights of the night, are increasingly rare and wonderful parts of human existence which most people cannot sense. Wouldn't it be great if this were a place where people could get back in touch with night?

26 AUGUST 1987

A now-aged copy of *The Jenguin Pennings* served as my introduction to the form I'm going to use here, but Bart Robinson's recent readings from *The Book of Liff* enlivened an otherwise dull evening of late. It is one of those games which can be played on a ledge à la "David" while waiting for a storm to pass.

The game is simple. The authors of *The Book of Liff* explain that numerous English words have but one purpose, to name places, so they have given those words definitions for situations which otherwise lack a name. Two of their examples: Ranfurley, *n.* a knot tying a cravat in such a manner that the narrow long end hangs below the stubby wide end; and Farrancassidy, *n.* a long, usually futile attempt by a member of one sex to release the catch on a brassiere usually being worn by a member of another sex.

Ranfurley happens to be the name of a village in Alberta, but that is a coincidence. Numerous other Alberta and British Columbia place names have dormantly been awaiting definition.

Stavely: *adj.*, tall and gracious, as a body borne on pins of limber pine. "She is a stavely woman, leaning slightly to port as if she had grown up tacking into the wind."

Rimbey: *adj.*, compensating with ethics what is lacking in morals. "How rimbey were 60s teenagers, always ready to protest racism and inequity, always pliant in one another's arms."

Midnapore: *n.*, a stage in life between the onset of middle age and its recognition. "He is a teacher in midnapore, still playing the Simon and Garfunkel and Bob Dylan records he had loved in his adolescence to his grade eights as examples of contemporary poetry;" or "Midnapore is undoubtedly upon her: but then she never should have worn a mini the first time around."

Didsbury: *n.*, a relationship or liaison between an older woman and a younger man. "They're always seen near cheap Bowness motels, but if you're mixed up in didsbury, that's what you have to do." Also *v.*, as in "He's didsburying."

Moving a bit close to home, we have the following:

Seebe: *adj.*, lacking insight, practicality, and precision. "His ideas are so seebe, like wanting to turn Bankhead into a golf course."

Laggan: *adj.*, at a two-league or six-kilometre remove from a major destination. "The business-residential district of Lake Louise is laggan."

Num-ti-jah: *n.*, a particular type of Rocky Mountain behaviour noted for its rootedness in the past, its swift vacillation between crustiness and graciousness.

Yoho: *interjection,* "'Yoho!' exclaimed the yahoo when he saw a yoyo."

Skoki: *adj.*, describing a type of voice both alluring and deceiving. "She shortened the wick of the coal oil lamp, then, looking at me with smoky eyes, said in a skoki voice: 'If you'll remove the wax from my skis, I'll make cocoa.'"

Kananaskis: *adj.*, smoochy in an obstreperous fashion. "He was nice enough in the bar, but when he gets you alone in the car he is so kananaskis."

Washmawapta: *v.*, to sluff and slew one's tires back and forth to get out of the snow. "We hadn't put the winter tires on yet, and had to washmawapta for a half-hour or more to get in the driveway.

Banff: *n.*, an excessive bribe. "I would have stayed for a week , but the landlord said, 'Don't you know the Olympics are coming up?' and he demanded a banff."

18 NOVEMBER 1987

My major venture into ice-carving came about on the eve of the Banff Winter Carnival the year I was in grade seven. The school provided the major tools – steel rakes and combs – and we gathered such hammers, screwdrivers, and pots to hold slush as we thought the job might require.

Miss Gratz lectured us on the seriousness of our endeavours. As I recall her words, she thought we should choose an animal subject simple in line and ready for abstraction. (No porcupines!) We should prepare drawings in advance and rough the subject out in profiles and then start eliminating everything that didn't look like what we were sculpting.

Thirteen year olds will be thirteen year olds. In my peer group that year *Destination Moon* was the popular movie. We wanted to create a moon rocket. Miss Gratz believed we should create something which would have more local significance. I would agree with her now, but at the time I thought she was way off-base.

Wild Animals of the World provided an otter which I thought she would think a suitable subject. Otters are sleek, graceful animals. Ice is a jagged, fracturing medium if you have little experience with it. Restoring shattered fragments is difficult if you must run back to the boys room in the high school to fetch sauce pans of water. Standish Service would have been handy but expedience wasn't our forte.

Meanwhile Nicky de Grandmaison was creating what we all agreed was a superlative mountain goat atop a promontory of rock (ice) in front of the Corner Drug Store, and Jim Davies was forming a crystalline seal with a ball balanced on his nose in front of the Robinson Clinic. Clever Jim! He hadn't listened to Miss Gratz with the same seriousness we had honoured her remarks with.

My otter wasn't very successful. It ended up looking a little like an upright three-toed Amazonian tree sloth or a terrified alley cat with its back arched. We had lost too much ice to give its tail anything like the thickness of an otter's tail and we never got the hang of reattaching slivers and shards of ice fragments. We would have done better to have carved a moon rocket or a pair of dice for all the talent we demonstrated in our neophyte carving careers.

Nicky's group spent hours on their mountain goat. They'd be out there for an hour before school started (at the civilized hour of nine o'clock then). They'd shape and add and subtract ice through lunch hour from noon until one-thirty. Then they'd be back working by street lights until eight in the evening.

Nicky's goat was a shoo-in for the big award, we all agreed. We didn't pay much attention to Jim Davies' circus seal. Miss Gratz had persuaded at least me that local imagery was the way to go.

We were shocked and dismayed therefore to learn that Jim's seal, which we had blithely ignored, was the big winner. We weren't the only ones unhappy with the judging.

Short hours after Jim's seal was given the laurel Nicky smashed his goat to rubble. Without a thought that a chinook and sunlight would reduce it to candle ice in a month or so, we thought it all such a waste.

3 FEBRUARY 1988

After his adventures in Connecticut, Walter Mitty got a job in Canada with Statistics Canada, so he immigrated to Paradise National Park.

"Alright, Mitty, we want to see what you're able to do, and we want to know what's going on in this place. The first thing you're going to do is look over that pile of reports, extract the necessary information from them, and tell us where we're leading the world."

Mitty bent to his task, as he began counting the reports – 1417 in 1987 alone – and realized Paradise National Park had created more reports per annum per capita than he had ever seen before, 0.26 reports per capita in a year, 246.7 reports per employee.

"Let's see," he murmured as he began his tabulations, his fingers flying over the keyboard of his computer "– per capita, per capita – 0.56 elk per capita, 0.023 T-shirt shops per capita, 0.019 gift shops per capita, 0.011 service stations per capita, per capita."

With all this information, thought Mitty, I can become one of the greatest tour escorts in Paradise National Park ...

He could already envision himself at the wheel of a tour bus.

He turned the key and heard the mighty cylinders in the engine compartment of the vehicle roar into action. "Capita per, capita per, capita per!"

"Welcome to Paradise National Park, per capita capital of the western world. Highest number of streets named for animals, highest number of hotels, hotel rooms, pillows, camp sites, hook-ups, RV sites per capita to be found anywhere in the civilized word. It's said that a citizen of Paradise – that's the administrative centre of Paradise National Park – would have a choice of nineteen beds to sleep in if all the rooms in town were empty – and he or she probably would, given the chance – and a lot of them were during the recent winter games. That's right, ma'am, more disgruntlement per capita than we've had before.

"That's the Paradise School of the Fine Arts up there on Excavation Hill. More administrators per capita than any other art school in the world, competing with the administration of Paradise Park I guess."

As he pushed the microphone aside, Mitty smiled to himself. "You should have been doing this years ago, Mitty," he said to himself. "This is what people really like. Facts and figures, per capita, per capita, are what keeps the world going. You're a statistician, Mitty, why didn't you figure this out before?"

"Mitty, what are you doing?"

Mitty grabbed the wheel. Just his luck to have a flat tire now, just when things were going so well, per capita-thunk, per capita-thunk.

"I've been watching you ten minutes now, and all you've done is clutch the sides of your keyboard and mumble 'per capita, per capita!' as though it means something. You've got ten minutes before your report is due. We get out one per capita per day, you know."

9 MARCH 1988

A major reward for living here is that just when the mountains start looking their best, the light becomes most wonderful, when people who have never put brush to paintpot begin considering a career as painters, and bright odours begin charging the atmosphere, nearly everyone who lacks a reason to be here goes home, and the place becomes nature's again. Nature's and ours.

Numerous photographs by Byron Harmon and many oil sketches by Belmore Browne and Carl Rungius celebrate this most magical of the year's times, the great festival of light which finally burns out like a fuzzy wick in the post-Thanksgiving storms. Those guys went out in the fall as often as in the summer and held on to the wilderness they loved until the threat of winter made them scurry and rush for home, taunting and teasing the season to see how close the first snaps of winter could come to their heels as they skedaddled down from the passes to the relative security of the valleys. A more daunting game when it could be four or five days travel to the highway or the railway.

The cloying scent of valerian, the acrid pungence of slowly rotting sedges, the oblique light and sharp shadow and resilience in our own muscles: from now until the creeks begin to freeze and the leaves have mostly fallen is the festival of the senses.

It's so easy to love the Rockies in July and August that the simplest of emotional types can believe he is a genius of response. As the days become tougher, and shaking off the chill of morning takes longer and longer, as the shrinking days remind of what it means to be Canadian, and autumn begins to make us pull our shoulders in a little tighter, our world becomes more rewarding for the time we spend in it.

In less than two months the air will have lost most of its heat, we shall strive to seek brighter areas for we know that only direct sunlight can keep us momentarily warm , and we'll scurry through the shadows.

Why then as the days grow shorter and dimmer and we know that the promise of bleak November shall certainly be made, why then does the world apparently become so much brighter? Brighter in the foliage, brighter in the contrast of the sunlit slopes and the deep mauves of the shadowed valleys of the mountains, brighter in the light that reflects from the river and through the silver and golden grass, and brighter in the clarity of the sharp scents that are subtler perfumes than the sexy scents of the bee and moth enticing flowers that so profligately wafted their way into the air as recently as a week ago.

Maybe it has something to do with quietness. As the motor homes and the tour buses retreat with their un-Canadian folk – and some Canadians in danger of losing their citizenship because they can't take it anymore! – the place becomes again the kind of quiet world we really want it to be. That is why it seems more correct, more rich, more private, more singlemindedly right than it does in the tumultuous periods of the year when the highway rumbles louder than the waterfall.

Perhaps it had to do with Bart Robinson's observation of twenty years ago when he first saw the wonderful light of autumn in the Canadian Rockies. "Never was light noisier," Bart later recalled. Did it have to do with the serenity and gentle quietness and all that terrifying oblique bright light?

31 AUGUST 1988

With evenings as warm as they have been, I've been sitting down on a bench by the river to listen to the concerts the elk are presenting on the far shore.

I don't own a sound sampler so I can only imagine the havoc I might create by taking a sample of their bugling and playing it back to them.

Can you imagine a bull elk suddenly hearing his last bugle played back to him but raised a tone or two? Suddenly shifted into C# minor?

"Hey, I thought I knew everybody in the valley. Who's the tenor? Everybody I know is a baritone!"

Robert Rosen, local composer, could really start shifting things around. Translate elk bugling into the choruses of Gabriele or some of that fabulous brass writing by Berlioz, like the *Tuba Mirum* in the Berlioz mass, and we'd have converging elk arriving from the Cascade, the Spray, Healy Creek, and Elk Lake joining in a glorious sound.

It would be as if a brigade of dudelsack players were to meet a battalion of sackbutters.

Add a couple of choruses of coyotes and Vivaldi in Heaven would be wondering how he managed to concentrate autumn into the simplicity of his concerto grosso.

Autumn's soundscape is so different from spring's. We may know that birdsong is not here for our entertainment but is really territorialism being announced loudly and clearly, although it doesn't sound like that.

In autumn birdsong begins to have different meanings. A couple of days ago I was ambling around the Fenland Trail, and while I was sitting on the bench by the beaver lodge I heard a gathering of mountain chickadees.

The chickadees' plaintive sounds of spring are silenced. Now the flock-forming cries dominate, the more familiar chickadee sounds. From now until February the little birds are going to be gathered together again. Their calling will keep the flock aware of its far-flung members.

Add the chickadee chorus to the coyotes and bugling elk, Mr. Rosen, and you'll keep your sampler busy, but with the right lyrics sung by the right alto, you'll have a song as haunting as those evocative recordings of howling wolves and singing whales.

Just to sit in the same place once a week for a year, to close your eyes and listen to the changing seasons is a wonderful cumulative experience.

It doesn't take much practice to believe that if you didn't know better, still you'd be able to wake from a Rip Van Winkle sleep and know within a week what time of year it is.

On a return trip to Banff a friend recently observed two things. One should be obvious to anyone: that Banff puts out a racket, now that it's grown too large, that he could hear all the way to the top of Tunnel Mountain.

The second thing he observed were the subtle differences between the sound of the wind in a coniferous forest and the sound of the wind in a deciduous forest. He didn't prefer the one to the other. It's just that he had never heard the differences so clearly before. (He was listening to the subtle things in order to not hear Banff's blasphemous brawling.)

Well, now that the revolution's here, we can pass sharply worded by-laws that will suppress unnecessary noise. If we're going to make this place liveable again, that's the type of restriction we're going to need. Nothing that drowns out the sound of chickadees, elk bugling, and coyotes will be permitted.

8 SEPTEMBER 1988

"It's snowing here," she whispered breathlessly into the telephone. "Can you tell me what's happening there? Can you rhapsodize a little?"

"Well," I said, "a white-breasted nuthatch is walking head-first down a black spruce, while a red squirrel is watching with an insouciant nonchalance which squirrels so rarely exhibit." I was trying to work as much colour into the sentence as possible. "The last golden leaves of the poplars are holding up well against the brightly blazoned blue sky."

"Hold it right there," she said. "Isn't it snowing?"

"We had a couple of centimetres overnight, but it's settled into a clear autumn day."

She was a CBC radio researcher in Calgary, phoning to get the word on the weather in the mountains. I was a solicited eloquence. Selected in hit-or-miss fashion from her list of contacts.

She wanted me to talk about the approach of winter, the "and what shall robin do then, poor thing" murmurings with which we lullaby naivety around us like a quilt. She wanted a sample of my improvisational abilities so she could write a question or two for Sharon Edwards who might talk to me later that day.

The bright blue sky would not wash.

"It isn't snowing up there?"

"Give it some time," I replied. "All our worst weather comes from Calgary, along with other undesirables, so if you've got a frontal disturbance, it might be here in four or five hours."

"What are you saying?"

"Well," I said, you know how difficult it is for Canadians to explain to Americans that all our worst weather comes from the U.S.? – all those storms that blow south from Michigan into Ontario, the dread blue southerners that whip into Montreal out of New York and

Vermont, and the killer storms that lay Manitoba and Saskatchewan low that are brewed in Montana and the Dakotas – all our worst weather in Banff comes out of a region that hovers somewhere over Coronation. We all know there's always weather in Coronation. Give us enough time, we'll get your weather too."

She phoned back later in the day – not quite so breathlessly – and was disheartened to learn that the sky was still blue, the light oblique, but the day unmercilessly bright. So I didn't get to talk to Sharon Edwards.

I was ready with enough material for a two-minute conversation, but no one in Calgary was going to hear my theories of autumn storms.

I'd talked with a former ski area operator, and his opinion was that any snow that fell before the 15th of October was merely a nuisance.

"It gets in the way and makes things slippery when you want dry ground to get things in order for the season, and it mucks things up. I always figured that snow that falls after the 15th of October is snow that is going to stay and it can be considered as potentially part of the winter snow pack.

"I remember one year when it was snowing in Calgary and my hill manager took a call from a Calgary radio station. Because there were flakes accumulating on the ground in the city, I guess they figured they'd get the jump on everybody else, and so one of the first questions they put to the hill manager – it must have been about the 10th of Ocotober – was 'when do you expect to have skiable snow?'

"He opened the window and put the phone out into the great outdoors, and in a voice loud enough for the announcer to hear, said, 'God, it's for you!'"

2 NOVEMBER 1988

"It is the day's dark midnight, and the year's," John Donne wrote. Then my memory plays a trick and I want to believe Donne went on to write, "Lucy's it is, when scant five hours the sun appears."

Is it six months since, on the other side of the sun, we took ourselves to Stoney Squaw's summit to behold the "day's bright noon tide and the year's? Sandford's day when eighteen hours the sun appears?"

Within an hour or two of our return from the Stoney Squaw prospect on June 21st, one of our number went to work at the Information Bureau. Within fifteen minutes a phone call came in from the wardens who said a grizzly mother and cub combination had been reported on Stoney Squaw that morning, and that the area was closed to hiking. Since we hadn't seen a sign of a bear, she thought it was a joke, but it was an authentic phone call from the wardens.

Lesley McNutt and her daughter had thought to join us for the dawnwatch, I learned two weeks later, but turned back when they saw the bear pair as they were driving up the hill. It was no joke.

Aside from the mosquitoes that morning, our dawn watch was a gentle way to celebrate an old-fashioned belief that aging children of the 60s – those with more faith in poetics than in astrophysics – have in Immanuel Velikovsky.

Now the day's dark midnight is here, the winter solstice and the beginning of the long cold, and we have rituals enough to implore the sun to come back to us.

We bring trees into our homes so we may know that all which is green is not gone forever. We light candles against the darkness, festoon trees with small points of light, starry gleams against the gloom and we sing the brightest traditional songs we know.

(Surprising, how surprising it is that people who otherwise deplore four-part harmony, despise melodies and airs of sublime richness and who barrage their ears with rock'n'roll, for ten or so days during the darkness of the year, respond to the possibilities of music.)

If I had to choose between participating in the rituals in the darkness to call back the sun, these revels in the solstitial gloom, and the rituals of the summer solstice, I'm sure winter's rites are more meaningful.

Three years ago in New Zealand I spent its longest day of the year atop a peak in Tongariro National Park. The long white cloud was so thick that day it didn't seem ritualistically significant that we stood on a mountain for the event. We did not see the sun that day.

Since Christmas combines folk and religious elements which concern the year's darkness, I wondered about its significance in the Southern Hemisphere.

Southern Hemisphere folks have no problems with Christmas at all. Like Californians and Texans, they accept fur-clad Santas, reindeer, lit-up evergreens and frost-covered Dickensian windows as what one sees in December. Then they go to the beach.

But a Wellington couple told me an increasing desire urging them to cast about in June's darkness for some type of event or ritual that will tie them to the movements of the planet as they see them from a prospect beneath the Southern Cross.

Light a candle now against the darkness. See the Hunter climb his way up into the sky. It is the day's dark midnight and the year's. Let our spirits brighten the winter night. Merry Christmas.

21 DECEMBER 1988

Ravens have been known to live as long as humans. We once fantasized capturing a raven, then teaching him to speak, to learn from him the ravens' point of view on the region's history. "He told you that? Liar. First person to ski to Assiniboine was Bill Peyto. I picked up scraps from his camp at Allenby Pass!"

Well, you get the idea. The ravens wouldn't have anything to gain or lose by telling us what they know.

Recently, however, we met a talking raven. We didn't ask him about history, mostly because we were so taken aback just by the mere fact of his talking. He did tell us more than we wanted to know about magpie culture. Understand, ravens are no admirers of magpies, so take the following with a grain of birdseed.

The first thing I asked the raven is what magpies talk about.

"What do magpies talk about?" he repeated. "Well, they're not philosophical like us ravens and crows. Caws and effect concern them not one whit. They spend much time in conversation that is little more than gossip. You wouldn't believe so much talk could result in so little being said of any importance. They spend a lot of time talking about hockey games."

"Hockey games?" I said.

"Hockey games. This time of year. Other times they talk about fashions and fads, rock and roll; then when the weather starts getting snappy in October they start talking about football, and then they talk about the weather."

"What are they so busy about all the time?" I asked.

"Well, when someone new moves into the neighborhood, they like to check him – or her – out. Look at her, they'll say, she thinks because she's got tail feathers like one of those African howdah birds, she's a peacock. That kind of activity keeps them busy."

"That's it?"

"They like to watch humans, too. I was talking to a pie the other day. We were checking out the new garbage containers. She was chattering so loudly I asked her to explain. She said all this human activity mystified her. Wanted to know about all your coming and going, all your running around, wanted to know what that building is where you all get together where there's so much arriving with pieces of paper and droppping them into a slot – which isn't a garbage container – then going in and coming out with new pieces of paper."

"The Post Office, you mean."

"I admit she has a point. We understand a lot about garbage, you understand, both the magpies and we ravens. But I can't understand, and neither could she, why you humans are so bound up in garbage which isn't even edible and never was."

"Seems like she was drifting into your territory, caws and effect."

"She could understand – though I can't – why you humans are beginning to look more and more like magpies," the raven said.

"We're beginning to look like magpies?"

"If you're not careful, you'll end up talking like parrots! She pointed out that you humans used to wear fairly drab colors, both summer and winter, though less of it in the summer. But over the past three or four years she's noticed you wear clothes with an iridescent sheen, just like magpie feathers, particularly when you go running and riding on bicycles."

"Lycra," I said.

"Whatever you say," he said. "Well, I've got to be going now."

"Why?" I shouted as he headed for a high tree to survey the fields.

"Be-caws. Be-caws. Be-caws!"

19 APRIL 1989

Unsolved Mysteries of the Canadian Rockies! Nature's strange secrets in Canada's park paradise!

The Green Spot of Stoney Squaw

Did a fiery meteorite sweep out of the sky in ancient days to scar forever the slopes of Stoney Squaw Mountain? Why do no trees grow on this mystifying meadow visible from time immemorial in the Bow Valley?

Is it true the Indians who moved through the valley for ten millennia used to seek their visions on this bald plate of a diminutive mountain? Is it true scientists who have investigated the soils of the Green Spot cannot say why grasses will grow on the slope but trees will not? Did visiting extra-terrestrials use it as a part of an ancient beacon system to tell them where the hot springs were ? Or where the flying saucer base is inside the hollow Mount Aylmer? Did hippy cults dance naked on the Green Spot during the summer solstice of 1968? Can one write this type of prose forever and not rely upon a single fact?

The Secret of the Cascade

Scientists have long wondered where the water from the cascade on Cascade Mountain goes after it enters the bowels of the Earth, another unsolved secret of the Canadian Rockies.

The Indians who camped at the base of the waterfall at Cascade Mountain which gives the mountain its name used to wonder where the water went after the stream plunged into the ground. They believed it was an entrance to the underworld and where the spirit went on its path to the happy hunting ground. The history of the cascade bewilders the scientists of today just as it puzzled the nomadic peoples of former centuries.

In the 1930s scientists dumped sawdust into the hole and posted people throughout the Bow Valley to see where the water came up.

When the test failed, they decided that dyeing the water would be a better way of determining the mysterious subterranean route of the stream.

Thousands of gallons of dye were poured into the foaming water and the earth accepted it all. Not one drop of coloured water was ever found to emerge on the surface of the valley.

Where does the water go? Will we ever know? Or will it be forever another *unsolved mystery of the Canadian Rockies?*

Mountain Lake has No Bottom!

Mysterious Lake Minnewanka in Banff National Park has confounded scientists from the earliest days of the lake's existence. Though it is contained in a defined valley, crews who have taken soundings on the lake have never determined the depth of the lake!

It is believed that huge ancient fish live in the murky depths of the lake, but they have never been recovered in a state suitable for scientists to investigate because they always explode in the reduced atmosphere at the surface.

Ten Year Old Boys Found to be Gullible!!

All three of the above "stories" were common when I was a kid. I hesitate to repeat them here now, for in our less sophisticated age (belief in horoscope equals lack of sophistication!) I'm sure that numerous readers of this paper are going to believe the intimations of the stories.

But I wonder if anyone wonders about the Green Spot or where the water from the Cascade goes or if Minnewanka has a bottom. These – and the source of the Hole-in-the-Wall – kept us intrigued for years.

3 May 1989

Rocky Mountain communities from Waterton to Prince George are certainly getting keen on celebrating the upcoming Marmot Day.

Marmot Day? On the day of the summer solstice, it is said, the energetic hiker who does not object to getting his feet wet may glimpse the great hoary marmot of the hills sticking his head out from his burrow to peer about to see if the eagles are flying overhead.

If, while he's looking for eagles, the marmot chances to see his shadow – a difficult thing for a marmot who is simultaneously wiping up to nine months' sleep from his eyes – we will have six more weeks of spring.

Six more weeks of spring! Think of it! Occasional snow storms, passing squalls, flooding creeks, chilly mornings, puddles and noisome clouds and quick winds, and the promise of summer held out like a perpetually receding bait!

Six more weeks of spring! And they can take us right to July's very end, when we can justifiably look to the sky and look at the thin clouds borne on the pale blue sky and sense the very first note of autumn in the richness of the afternoon.

So there exists the merest chance the great hoary marmot will not see his shadow when on the solstice he sticks his head out from the rock pile, and in that event – and this is why hikers take themselves to the edge of the meadows in late June – we shall actually have a summer.

Pshaw! on your Groundhog Day, ye easterners who live in groundhog country. Need a possibility of six more weeks of winter concern ye when winter has sat upon thy doorstep six weeks only from the day of the equinox, and there is legitimate reason to believe there may yet be six more weeks of winter?

But to have endured three full months of spring as we have in the mountains, days of unsettled direction and weeks when an onslaught of cold repels each advance of warmth, and then to have the hoary marmot see his shadow, to know storm and snow will nip the darling buds of May, and will continue into June, the very end of spring, and continue forty days more!

This is to break the heart, to dampen spirit, quench the soul, darken the sills of the eyes, and make our minds despair.

Attentive eyes watch the marmot as he nuzzles his hoary muzzle over his home's rocky sill, and weary minds hope the day of the solstice is overcast, for the cost of the marmot's shadow is so dear.

He blinks. He squints. He backs up from the dazzle of the daylight and shudders to return to his nine months' dreams of whatever it is marmots dream of. But his stomach's gnawing tells him he must draw deep the draught of air of spring, and warily move out to the small shoots of green grass.

Earnest hearts have hoped the cloud will linger longer in the path of the sunbeams, while the marmot nuzzles the pale green shoots. But two years out of three the sun will not stay hid, and the marmot beholds his great head's bulk in shadow on the grass.

One year in three the marmot does not see his shadow and then we are blessed with full six weeks of summer before the chill winds begin to make their way down from the glaciers and frosts clasp the ground again.

Now you can understand, surely, why we mountain people make so much of Marmot Day!

14 JUNE 1989

As surely as it is September, summer having two weeks yet to run before the equinox, we will soon hear talk of skiing.

It's difficult to persuade those people who do not know the year has four seasons that skiing the Canadian Rockies does not begin the day after summer is over, nor that we residents of the Rockies relish these shoulders of the seasons in which we can saunter, amble, and otherwise enjoy the very reasons we choose to live here. Late September and early October: let's keep them for ourselves.

I hear talk an effort is soon to be made to attract people to come here in November. It won't be an easy month to sell.

In my mind's eye I can see the promotional literature now. "Visit the Canadian Rockies in November! Experience new shades of grey! See one of Nature's rarest spectacles: watch ice form on rivers, streams, and creeks! Behold the removal of life from the world! Experience Nature's closest resemblance to the effects of nuclear winter!"

All Hallows' Day (November 1st) always seems among the greyest days of the year, but after it several long weeks drag with caterpillar pace toward winter solstice. They are nearly always snow-free and dull weeks.

Henry David Thoreau, the most important philosopher to emerge from the United States, argues that one can tell the true nature lover by the manner in which he loves the year's marginal months.

If you see sojourners on the edges of Vermilion Lakes in late November awaiting the swans on their brief stay as they come in from the Arctic world, if you see wanderers among the the barren aspen trees on Mt. Edith's lower slopes, chances are you are beholding nature's true lovers.

The natural world is easy to love in May when new leaves are emerging. The bounty of August, September and October is admirable, and maturation and maturity surround us with ripeness and meaning.

But the Chamber of Commerce has its work cut out for it if it hopes to make festivals of leaf mould, leaden skies and pewter clouds, frozen ponds, crushed grass, darkness and dusk.

Summer nights and meteor showers, the dropping into the night of bats from poplar trees, the clash of antlers on the the further shores of the Bow, the haunting music of elk bugling, the long autumnal migrating bighorn rams: these are spectacles worth attending.

But November? Come to see and hear coyotes call to diesel locomotives! See Banffites escape to urban fleshpots! Encounter boredom at its thickest.

It is easy to take delight in watching children run about catching snowflakes on their tongues. It is wonderful to "watch the woods fill up with snow," but it is not so easy to take the days in which skiers too soon anticipating the possibility of skiable snow attend every storm front as though it be the meaningful one.

But we move apace too quickly, don't we? Two weeks of summer, and then four weeks of golden autumn await us, including that usually wonderful week after Thanksgiving, when the world is ours and easy to take pleasure in.

Then eight or nine weeks pass until the days when we can usually anticipate snow on the ground. We have no need to rush things.

Snappy air, its sharper edge on skin, the silent streets, the deeper nights, the return of the Hunter to the sky over Rundle: these are not the types of topic we make attractions of for others, but they have their own pleasure for us, just in their tuning us to the world around us.

7 SEPTEMBER 1989

How and where Bruce Beattie recently met Eddie Evans, we will never be exactly sure, but, upon meeting, the two late Banffites greeted each other as long-lost friends.

In tones similar to the sound of a slurry of gravel in a placer box, Bruce asked Eddie, "How have you been?"

"Parched," Eddie replied. "It don't matter where I wander about this place, I can't find a place where a gentleman can sit down and order a couple of glasses of draft. Sometimes I think I could wring the necks of the attendants. They just don't seem to care."

"My sentiments exactly," Bruce said. "I thought I had the bases covered. If it were to be Heaven, I thought fountains of lager would pour from the very clouds; and were it to be Hell, I thought the Devil would surely provide his charges with the demon booze."

"I've checked it out pretty well," said Eddie. "There's not a drop to be had. You know, I'd like to be back in Banff again."

A cloud suddenly enclosed the two chaps, their vision darkened and they felt themselves accelerating into space.

"I haven't felt anything like this since I rode the cab of a 5900 plunging into the Upper Spiral Tunnel. Whoopee!"

The cloud settled the twirling pair down on terra firma, their eyes slowly adapting to the brilliance of the shimmering lights of the shops towering three storeys into the night. Eddie said, "It may be Banff, Bruce, but it don't look like the town I grew up in. It don't look quite right. I don't remember this many Japanese signs."

"Oh, you'll get used to them, Eddie. You weren't around in the 80s, so you don't know about that. But some things'll never change. I'll get me bearings in a moment. Aha, there's the Cascade Service Station and the high school, the Presbyterian church. Now where's the Standish Hardware? I don't recognize that big building where the B-J Novelty used to be, but it isn't Maria Stenton we're looking for now, is it? The place we're looking for will never change. Mind the sidewalk, Eddie, they've taken the sharp edges off them at the corners so the kids can ride their bikes right up on to them. It can unsettle a fellow the first couple of times."

The two friends ambled south along the 200 block of Banff Avenue.

"I kind of miss the Firehall on Banff Avenue," Eddie said.

"Keep up that nostalgia, you're going to be missing the telephone offices next door," Bruce said. "They've been gone for a while too."

When they reached the Dominion Cafe (once upon a time the National aka the Red Hat, Great Expectations, Mr C's, Tommy's) Eddie set a faster pace. "C'mon Brucie, shake a leg!"

"Eddie, look!"

"What?"

"There ain't no Eddy, Eddie."

"Cut the joking, Bruce."

"I'm not joking, there's no bricks, no door, there isn't even a floor. Tell me it isn't so. There isn't even a Don. The Eddy isn't."

"I don't like this, Bruce."

"Well, there's still the Cascade. There'll always be the Cascade!"

"Where's the Lux Theatre, Bruce? You sure this is Banff?"

"You can't stop progress, Eddie. You can't stop progress."

"Bruce, where's the door to the Cascade?"

"Where's the Cascade is more to the point!"

"Whose idea was this Bruce?"

"Well, if we can't get a beer, I guess we'll just have to go to the Banff Cafe, settle for a coffee, and I'll tinkle the old ivories."

"Bruce, don't look now, but there isn't a Banff Cafe."

"We'd better go back to where we were." Another cloud swirled upon them and bore them away.

4 JANUARY 1990

When the temperature fell to twenty-five or thirty below (Fahrenheit) for the first day of any winter, there was always an argument over the breakfast table about whether we should go to school or not.

Drop the temperature way below zero, give the dread blue norther enough oomph and push, and Tom Dunsmore, the Banff Elementary School janitor, found it impossible to keep the heating system in the old elementary school up and running.

That was about five years before natural gas came to town, so heating throughout the town was done by coal. Keeping a boiler up and running on a day when a storm was raging must have been exceedingly hard work, requiring the stamina of a locomotive fireman.

It was a marginal game though. We had to bundle up and move out into the teeth of a storm. (Only the very rare kid got a ride to school in the 40s and 50s; either the kid or his parents were chicken.) We had to move slowly enough to keep upright, but fast enough not to end up with frostbite circles on our cheeks.

If the day was adequately cold, it would take about ten minutes for Billy A. and Tom to agree that Tom would never get the boiler up to full, and the word would go out that "the boiler had broken," and we would be given the rest of the day off.

You can understand therefore why walking to school was important: if we hadn't walked to school, then when it was too cold for school and school was cancelled, we couldn't play outside all day.

But there was a slight chance, of course, that Tom would get the temperature up and therefore we had to go to school just in case.

Only once can I remember a storm turning me back.

The blizzard of 1948 had raged all through the night. By the time dawn's faint light had turned the world a pale blue it was also time to go out into the whistling mournful morning.

I followed the path broken by my cousin Donny who was wearing flight boots and a flight jacket – de rigueur style for high school kids in that era. It was okay going through the hedge-protected yard of my grandmother's house, but on Bear Street the wind developed hurricane force, and I couldn't keep up with Donny, who lowered his head like a prairie buffalo and pushed right on.

By the time we reached the White Owl, turning on to Caribou Street, he was already fifty or sixty feet ahead of me, his forward motion propelling him ahead at a pace I couldn't keep up with.

With relief I paused for a moment to watch wind swirls overtake his form and engulf him, then turned back into the trough in the snow the two of us had made.

With the wind at my back, the retreat to home was fairly easy. I was probably out in the storm for six or seven minutes by the time I got back home. Within a half hour, Donny and my sister and brothers were back home too.

"The boiler's bust," was the word.

That storm was one of the two great storms I remember here. The wind raged all through the day, and the temperature continued to drop.

My memory, likely not accurate in all the details, says that was the occasion when the temperature went right down to sixty below the following night, and school was cancelled for two days rather than the usual one.

31 JANUARY 1990

My cousin Cliff and I took our skis off to ascend Deception Pass. It was easier to walk on the solid enough skidoo track than to keep our skis on. We noticed a woman and an older man apparently engaged in wax talk on the slope below Carson Peak. About the time we took our skis off, they started out and made good regular time up the slope.

His kickturns and switchbacks brought the man to our elevation fifty or so metres below the pass. "Nice day," he said. "About the nicest I can recall in my trips to Skoki," I said, "but speaking for myself only." Pointing to Cliff, I said, "He has made many more trips to Skoki than I have."

"Sam Evans," the man said, identifying himself. We identified ourselves. "We are much honored," I said, "to be at Skoki when you are." Then he took off for one last small switchback. I dashed ahead to snap a picture of Cliff and Sam together. As Sam approached Cliff again, he said, "You'd be young Cliff White then, wouldn't you." These days Cliff rarely meets people who skied to Skoki before him.

Sam's part in skiing in the Rockies goes back to the early 30s when he made his first trip to Assiniboine, and in the later 30s he and Ken Jones packed hundreds of pounds of supplies per week into Skoki when Jim Boyce was running the lodge.

Sam, 79 on March 21st, and his daughter were skiing out to Skoki to meet up with 79.4-year-old Ken Jones. The following day the two men, both in their eightieth years, skied to the top of Merlin Ridge above Merlin Lake.

Ken told us he had made his first pair of skis when he was a school kid in Golden. Learned about skis from some Swedish kids in the town who sailed over the snow to the envy of the kids on snowshoes.

His answers to our questions about wax brought an astonishing reply. The Swedish kids, he said, used to apply salt herring to the bottom surfaces of their skis. "There was enough fat in the herring to act as wax."

The weekend brought another living legend of the Rockies back to Banff. Murray Adaskin, now 84, one of Canada's finest and best-known composers, played with the Toronto Trio at the Banff Springs Hotel for the summers of the 1930s.

Murray on violin, Louis Crerar on piano, and Cornelius Ysselstyn on cello developed an immense repertoire for those summers in Banff. Because many guests were here the entire summer, the trio didn't want to repeat pieces in their evening concerts in the Mt. Stephen Hall. (Concerts every evening except Thursday: Dan McCowan gave a natural history talk that evening.)

I asked Murray if he had ever played St. George's bells. "No," he said, then gave the question a moment more thought. "Once," he said. "The parson was very proud of them and he asked me to look at them so I went up the tower with him.

"He played a tune or two, to show me how, then asked me if I wanted to play something.

"I knew Louis Crerar was in town so I played a little tag which all musicians know." He whistled it, saying, "It means 'Clear the room, here's a horse's ass.'

"Louis was in town returning a seltzer bottle for the deposit. When he heard that familiar secular refrain on the bells, it startled him so, he dropped the bottle and it exploded."

4 APRIL 1990

This is not an urban legend. Nor is it a rural legend.

It bears no relationship to the type of story in which a woman spends too long in a tanning salon and dies because she has cooked her insides.

Nor is it akin to the cautionary tale in which a ready-mix man drives home in the afternoon in his loaded truck and, seeing his best friend's convertible outside his house, thinks some hanky-panky is going on, unloads a yard of aggregate into an open Miata.

It begins with a simple lapse. A woman walks her dog up Tunnel Mountain. (Breed of dog unknown; the imagination supplies some details: a small, yappy dog.)

Maybe the dog was never on a leash. It should have been on a leash.

Dog gets too close to the cliff side of the top of the mountain. One way or another the dog falls off the top of the mountain. Woman is distressed.

Two gallant men, ages unknown, happen by and hear the woman's sad tale, how the dog got too close to the edge and disappeared. She thinks it may have fallen right to the bottom.

(My "facts" may but approximate the truth, but I doubt that the principals in the story will come forward to correct me.)

Holding on to the branches of trees, the men take a gander off the top of the mountain, and see nothing.

But they are gallant.

They tell the woman that it may be possible that the dog is somewhere at the bottom of the mountain, so they head on down the trail. Above the summer school they turn along Tunnel Mountain Road and take the trail that leads from Bow Falls to the Hoodoos.

When the trail reaches the base of the mountain they move along the margin of trees at the bottom of the cliffs. They find nothing.

"Maybe," one of them suggests, "the dog got caught up on one of those trees a little higher up. Maybe we should go and check."

So, not too adept at climbing, but enthusiastic and gallant, they start climbing up the mountain, holding on to branches and tree trunks, using such technical aids as the mountain offers up naturally.

They eventually reach a point about two thirds of the way up the back of the mountain where they find their way is blocked. They can proceed no further. Nor do they have the skills to retreat.

Stuck.

They light a fire to signal golfers to their plight.

Eventually, about 6 or 7 pm their fire is spotted, and word reaches the wardens.

It takes a while to check out the situation, to assemble a rescue team in the September dusk, but finally, lit by the glow of a Coleman lamp, seven wardens – Stretchy, Elk-smeller, Spandex, Wheezie, Woodsy, Clamber, Et Cetera – set up the rescue and by 11:30 or midnight, the two dog-rescuers have been themselves rescued by the full team of dog-rescuer-rescuers and pulled up to the top of the mountain by the harness and rope technique.

We don't know what has happened to the distressed woman whose dog precipitated this mayhem, but the end of the story is that the fire started by the two dog-rescuers to attract the attention to themselves turned into a small conflagration covering about forty or fifty square feet, and it needs attention itself, since wardens are not yet used to turning their back on forest fires.

The dog has not been found.

11 OCTOBER 1990

I don't know if this is column #1000 but it's closing in on the millennium. It got started in the *Crag* in the years when Stephanie and Pat Boswell bought and improved the *Crag*, when the newspaper occupied the space where Banff Park Printing and The Sunflower are now located. Editors, seven or eight of them over the years, more of them in the earliest and latest years, revolved in and out of a cubbyhole that served as an office, ownership changed once, and the office moved further down Bear Street.

Lizzie Rummel suggested the column title, which came from a letter to her from Arnold Brigden of Winnipeg who quoted a couplet by William Blake: "Great things occur when men and mountains meet;/This seldom happens when passing in the street."

When Georgia Engelhard Cromwell, one of the two greatest female alpinists in Canada (the other was the late Phyllis Munday), died a few years back, I changed the name to reflect the perceptions which the feminist revolution changed and improved.

I have been twice threatened by law suits for items I wrote about here. It would be impolitic to rehash details now, thrashing long dead horses anew, but the issues I raised which caused those threats were both reconciled in ways which resulted in addressing and correcting the wrongs I had identified.

I've found the time, occasion, and impulse to write, co-write and publish sixteen or seventeen books over the years, while editing many more, and stimulating most of the revolution in authorship which has occurred in the Bow Valley. If the quality of information visitors to Banff and its three adjacent national parks now receive is better and more accurate than it was 20 years ago – and I think it is – it is largely because I zealously praised that which was well done while deploring the shoddy, hapless research sometimes passed off because "it's only a book for tourists."

I haven't been able to keep up to the violences done to the valley, the town, and the community by the constantly gathering forces of darkness. In the past ten years we have seen a few improvements – the refurbishment of the Bow River Bridge stands out, for example – but the excesses of growth, allowed by national park administration and the Banff Advisory Council, have poisoned the perception of Banff forever.

The ledger can make one feel useless. Twenty years ago, the balance of summer and winter visitation, facilities and housing, and services and demand was even, and the town had a healthy sensibility. How did matters get so out of shape? How did the community of Banff allow itself to be so weak-willed that it did not rise up again and again against the villainies and injustices which I and so many other people felt were eroding the spirit of the town?

Had I written about each nick of the death of a thousand nicks – while recognizing that some of them have been swipes, gashes, slashes, gouges, and lacerations – that have weakened the Banff that used to be, I would not have had time to reflect on the real joys that can exist here.

But it's all over now. This is my last column for a while. Now I'm going to take some time out to figure out why matters deteriorated in the 1970s and 80s, and why such an ethical and moral vacuum developed here. The only way I know how to find out such matters is to dig more deeply into the record than I have been able to hitherto.

21 FEBRUARY 1991